DIEGO FOSSATI,
NICHOLAS THOMAS, AND
MARK THOMPSON

TOWARDS INCLUSIVE SOCIAL POLICIES?

Southeast Asia after the Pandemic

AF071322

POLICY PRESS SHORTS RESEARCH

First published in Great Britain in 2025 by

Policy Press, an imprint of
Bristol University Press
University of Bristol
1–9 Old Park Hill
Bristol
BS2 8BB
UK
t: +44 (0)117 374 6645
e: bup-info@bristol.ac.uk

Details of international sales and distribution partners are available at
policy.bristoluniversitypress.co.uk

© Diego Fossati, Nicholas Thomas, and Mark Thompson 2025

The digital PDF and ePub versions of this title are available open access and distributed under the terms of the Creative Commons Attribution-NonCommercial-NoDerivatives 4.0 International licence (https://creativecommons.org/licenses/by-nc-nd/4.0/) which permits reproduction and distribution for non-commercial use without further permission provided the original work is attributed.

DOI: 10.51952/9781447376255

British Library Cataloguing in Publication Data
A catalogue record for this book is available from the British Library

ISBN 978-1-4473-7623-1 paperback
ISBN 978-1-4473-7624-8 ePub
ISBN 978-1-4473-7625-5 OA Pdf

The right of Diego Fossati, Nicholas Thomas, and Mark Thompson to be identified as authors of this work has been asserted by them in accordance with the Copyright, Designs and Patents Act 1988.

All rights reserved: no part of this publication may be reproduced, stored in a retrieval system, or transmitted in any form or by any means, electronic, mechanical, photocopying, recording, or otherwise without the prior permission of Bristol University Press.

Every reasonable effort has been made to obtain permission to reproduce copyrighted material. If, however, anyone knows of an oversight, please contact the publisher.

The statements and opinions contained within this publication are solely those of the authors and not of the University of Bristol or Bristol University Press. The University of Bristol and Bristol University Press disclaim responsibility for any injury to persons or property resulting from any material published in this publication.

Bristol University Press and Policy Press work to counter discrimination on grounds of gender, race, disability, age and sexuality.

Cover design: Chris Wilson
Front cover image: Shutterstock/KenSoftTH
Bristol University Press and Policy Press use environmentally responsible print partners.
Printed and bound in Great Britain by CPI Group (UK) Ltd, Croydon, CR0 4YY

Bristol University Press' authorised representative in the European Union is: Easy Access System Europe, Mustamäe tee 50, 10621 Tallinn, Estonia,
Email: gpsr.requests@easproject.com

Contents

List of tables and figures		iv
Acknowledgements		v
one	Taking stock of the pandemic in Southeast Asia	1
two	Theorising possibilities of change	25
three	Attitudinal and behavioural change	44
four	Institutions, politics, and social welfare	76
five	Outcomes and implications	101
Appendix: Sociodemographic composition of the five samples		115
Notes		119
References		120
Index		145

List of tables and figures

Tables
1.1	COVID-19 cases in Southeast Asia (as of 5 March 2023)	18
3.1	Descriptive statistics for the variables in the survey	50
3.2	Perceived change in support for various social policies	54
3.3	Determinants of attitudinal change in five countries	60
3.4	Determinants of behavioural change in five countries	71

Figures
1.1	Institutional trust in five Southeast Asian countries	13
3.1	Increased support for social policies in five countries	56
3.2	Change in support for international cooperation in healthcare	57
3.3	Change in support for social policy among different sociodemographic groups	59
3.4	Support for economic redistribution and attitudinal change	66
3.5	Change in four behaviours as a result of COVID-19	68
3.6	Anxiety about infection and behavioural change	73

Acknowledgements

Data collection and analysis for this monograph was fully funded by Hong Kong's University Grants Committee General Research Fund Grant (GRF) 11610021, awarded to Diego Fossati (Principal investigator), Nicholas Thomas (Co-investigator), and Mark Thompson (Co-investigator). The authors are grateful to Samuel Lai for excellent research assistance. Teh Hui Wen, Annanya Guha, Han Jonghee, and Zhang Yuhan assisted as well.

ONE

Taking stock of the pandemic in Southeast Asia

Major events and crises are known for their potential to foster change, but the extent and impact of the change is only understood after the crisis is resolved. Whenever a crisis emerges, the assumption is that the urgent need to address specific issues becomes even more pronounced, learning processes are expedited, public demand for reform strengthens, and political divisions may be temporarily bridged with the policy changes undertaken (Kamkhaji and Radaelli, 2017). However, alongside these reactive changes are more conservative aspects of governance. When it comes to policy responses to crises, change can be problematic due to the 'stickiness' of existing institutions, processes of path dependence, the marginalisation of potential agents of change, and the presence of powerful veto players (Boettke et al, 2015).

In this book, we analyse the COVID-19 pandemic through these competing lenses and with a particular focus on Southeast Asia. We ask whether, and to what extent, the significant disruptions caused by the pandemic led to meaningful shifts in both public preferences on social policies and the development of welfare state institutions in this region. We particularly seek to use this analysis to ask why these shifts did or did not occur. In exploring these questions, we employ a mixed-methods approach, combining quantitative surveys on public attitudes with qualitative case studies of institutional change in key Southeast Asian countries. This allows us to capture both broad patterns of attitudinal shifts and the particular institutional responses that vary across national contexts. Our analysis contributes to the broader literature on crisis-driven policy change by offering new insights into how major crises like COVID-19 can reshape public preferences and institutional frameworks in non-Western contexts, which have been comparatively underexplored in existing scholarship.

In this chapter, we provide essential background information on Southeast Asia that will be crucial for contextualising the analysis of attitudinal and institutional change in Chapters 3 and 4. We start with an overview of the argument of the book and a discussion of its contributions to existing research. Then, we examine political institutions in Southeast Asia, with a particular focus on state formation, regime types, and the development of welfare states. We go on to look at the historical legacies of infectious diseases in the region, policy responses to these health crises, and how they have influenced the evolution of health policies. Next, we analyse the responses to COVID-19 across Southeast Asia, paying special attention to the varying ways countries balanced economic, political, and epidemiological concerns. Finally, we provide an overview of the book's structure and key arguments.

Background, argument, and contribution

COVID-19 is an apt illustration of a disruptive crisis that can facilitate policy change. First, the pandemic exposed vulnerabilities and inefficiencies in public health systems worldwide, leading to a re-evaluation of healthcare policies, funding, and preparedness (Lal et al, 2021). Governments generally responded quickly and vigorously as they implemented measures like emergency stimulus packages, increased healthcare funding, and a focus on vaccine research and distribution, thereby altering the trajectory of the pandemic. Second, and more broadly, COVID-19 laid bare the fragility of economic and social safety nets, especially for marginalised and low-income populations. The scale of economic disruption led to discussions of policies such as the provision of a universal basic income, expanded unemployment benefits, and more robust social support systems. This crisis appeared to open a window of opportunity for social policy reform and raised the possibility of increased public demand for stronger protections and safety nets for future shocks (Curtice, 2020).

Given this window of opportunity, has the COVID-19 pandemic facilitated the adoption of more generous and inclusive social policies? To be sure, it may be too early to offer a conclusive answer this question. Yet most of the initial evidence indicates that the global pandemic has only changed public perceptions and policies to a limited extent. Scholarship on public opinion has generally emphasised the continuity in public attitudes on social policy. For example, some studies have argued that increases in support for social policies such as expanded economic benefits and family support were only temporary (Ebbinghaus et al, 2022), and public support for economic redistribution or more radical policies such as universal basic income still varies along sharp ideological and partisan divides (Tonelli et al, 2024).

Many scholars have also been sceptical of the transformative impact of COVID-19 on social policy making. As mentioned earlier, governments took prompt and substantial policy measures during the early phases of the pandemic, and the pandemic has generated a lively debate, both in academia and policy circles, on possible changes and new directions in social policy (Natali, 2022). Yet, most extant research understands these policies as exceptional measures to counter unprecedented social and economic upheaval rather than long-lasting moves to expand and strengthen the social safety net.

For example, some have argued that while the pandemic has accelerated some changes that were already underway, it has not facilitated deeper policy reform and most implemented policies relied on existing pre-pandemic tools and national policies (Béland et al, 2021a). Most importantly, to echo the findings of a recent review (Cruz-Martínez et al, 2023), there is substantial variation across countries in the degree to which COVID-19 policies have been institutionalised, which could be explained by variation in factors such as prevailing policy framing and previous welfare state development legacies (Cantillon et al, 2021).

While the extensive body of literature on the implications of COVID-19 has yielded valuable insights, it predominantly reflects the experiences of Western countries and focuses largely on the acute phase of the crisis. As a result, we know far less about how the pandemic influenced public attitudes and policies in non-Western nations and less-developed economies. These regions, where welfare state institutions are often markedly different and, in most cases, less developed when compared to those in advanced economies, offer a critical yet understudied context for examining the long-term effects of the pandemic. Now that the acute phase has transitioned into a more stabilised 'new normal', we may ask if, and to what extent, COVID-19 triggered a process of lasting transformation in welfare institutions within these countries. This question is particularly important given that many of these nations were already grappling with limited social safety nets and institutional capacity before the pandemic.

We propose to address this question with a study of five countries in Southeast Asia, a region that, as we further elaborate in the next sections of this chapter, provides ideal ground for this study thanks to its heterogeneity in domestic politics, welfare state institutions, socioeconomic development, and experiences with the pandemic. To study attitudinal change, we undertook original opinion surveys in Indonesia, Malaysia, the Philippines, Singapore, and Thailand asking respondents about their views of social policy and how these have changed because of the pandemic. To study institutional change, we conducted qualitative studies of the same five countries, focusing on policy responses to the pandemic, their degree of institutionalisation, and patterns of policy convergence and divergence across countries.

By focusing on Southeast Asia and jointly analysing both attitudinal and institutional change, we offer three main contributions to existing research. First, we document with our original surveys that many Southeast Asians perceive the pandemic as a transformative event. More than five years after the onset of COVID-19, a substantial share of our respondents reported having changed their views and preferences on social policy issues such as the role of the state in healthcare, provision of unemployment benefits, and health insurance as well as, in some cases, their attitudes towards broader fiscal issues such as economic redistribution. While we also document important differences across social groups and countries, this finding suggests substantial support for policy change among Southeast Asian publics. Given this attitudinal change, the pandemic may indeed have constituted an opportunity to significantly expand existing social safety nets in the region.

Second, we identify a mismatch between attitudinal and institutional change. While many Southeast Asians may have changed their minds about important social policy issues, having become more acceptant and expectant of more generous social policies and welfare state arrangements, we have found limited responsiveness to this change among political elites and institutions. Governments in the region did respond forcefully to the pandemic emergency, motivated by the two paramount, and often conflicting, goals of limiting infections and deaths while minimising economic disruptions. Yet, after the end of the acute phase of the pandemic, expanded welfare measures were largely phased out, and no influential political actors in the region have since consistently advocated for a permanent expansion of existing social insurance policies or increased economic redistribution.

Finally, we explain this gap between citizens and political elites by examining the role of historical legacies of state formation and welfare state development in the region as well as more recent political dynamics. We argue that the reason why increased support for broader social policies has not materialised into policy change can be traced in part to the institutional legacies of authoritarian state formation, during which the political Left have been systematically repressed, thereby suppressing actors such as labour unions and progressive parties that typically advocate for welfare state expansion (Hewison and Rodan, 2011). Yet the political vacuum created by the repression of pro-socialist forces in the region was often filled by highly mobilised civil societies, albeit with recurrent competition between liberal and illiberal forces within them. Progressive-leaning activists rode the democratisation wave across the region from the mid-1980s, but democratic backsliding has eroded the influence of civil society in the region. This has frequently weakened activist groups as well as led to the marginalisation or co-optation of opposition parties, excluding them as potential 'change agents' in the Southeast Asian countries considered in this study.

Related to this, welfare state institutions in Southeast Asia, despite broad-based support for egalitarian values in public opinion (Fossati and Martinez i Coma, 2023), have developed within a conservative ideological climate characterised by a strong anti-welfarist and a neoliberal productivist discourse that prioritises economic growth and labour market participation over social protection. This political, institutional, and ideological environment has reinforced the notion that state support should be minimal and contingent on productivity, further constraining the space for progressive social policy reforms.

Additionally, in some countries in the region, populism, clientelism, and political instability have played a significant role in shaping welfare policy outcomes. Like elsewhere in the world, populist politicians, particularly in Indonesia and the Philippines, have exercised power with limited accountability, and this was particularly evident during the pandemic, when their popularity remained high despite blatant mistakes in dealing with the crisis (Hapal, 2021; Thompson, 2022). Relatedly, political elites in the region have often relied on patronage networks to maintain power and distributed selective benefits to loyal supporters rather than developing universal welfare programmes. This patronage approach has not only undermined the potential for comprehensive social policy but also perpetuated inequality and limited the state's capacity to implement broad-based welfare reforms (Blunt et al, 2012).

Moreover, political instability in countries such as Malaysia and Thailand has further hindered the development of durable welfare institutions, as frequent regime changes and shifting political alliances have created a volatile environment that discourages long-term planning and policy innovation. In Singapore, the need for massive, short-term social assistance during COVID-19 did not lead to the ruling People's Action Party (PAP) abandoning its ideological hostility to welfarism, and it quickly discontinued most social welfare measures after the pandemic eased, in the name of restoring fiscal stability (International Monetary Fund [IMF], 2023). Together, these factors have reinforced the persistence of limited welfare provision despite public opinion shifting in favour of expanded social protection.

This book offers a novel contribution to the research on COVID-19 in Southeast Asia by integrating public policy analysis with a focus on political dynamics in the five countries we analyse. While existing works such as Sciortino's (2023) edited volume on the pandemic's impact on economic inequality and marginalised groups and Shin et al's (2022) multidisciplinary review of social and economic policies provide important insights, they focus primarily on the immediate public policy outcomes of the pandemic. In contrast, our book extends beyond these frameworks by incorporating an analysis of political dynamics, both in terms of immediate political responses to the crisis and the influence of historical legacies on contemporary policy making. Additionally, our research uses original survey data to examine how the general public, rather than just marginalised groups, has shaped and responded to welfare state changes. Other works, such as Aslam and Gunaratna's (2022) wide-ranging collection and Tan and Chan's (2023) analysis of demographic shifts, also offer valuable contributions, but our book provides an analysis that bridges public policy with political institutions and legacies. By doing so, we believe this volume offers a deeper understanding as to how the pandemic not only influenced policy making but also (re)shaped the political landscape in Southeast Asia.

Southeast Asia's institutional context

Southeast Asia is a particularly suitable region for a study of how the COVID-19 pandemic may have altered public attitudes towards social policy and influenced the expansion of social policy programmes and institutions. As mentioned earlier, much of the existing research on the pandemic's impact has focused on Western countries, and non-Western contexts such as Southeast Asia remain comparatively understudied. This deficit in the literature presents an opportunity to examine how the pandemic has affected public opinion and institutional development in regions with markedly different political, economic, and social configurations from those of advanced economies.

Indeed, many Southeast Asian cases differ from Western and advanced economies along several relevant dimensions. First, welfare state institutions in the region are distinctive from those in many advanced economies, although welfare state regimes in the West vary, ranging from liberal to more encompassing, social democratic models (Esping-Andersen, 1990). Compared with most Western cases, the development of social policy institutions in Southeast Asia has been relatively limited and uneven. While the difference is sometimes overstated (Hort and Kuhnle, 2000), welfare state provisions in this region tend to be less comprehensive and more fragmented, with a stronger emphasis on informal safety nets, family-based support systems, and targeted assistance programmes than on universal social security (Croissant, 2004; Aspalter, 2006). This contrast offers an opportunity to explore how a major global crisis like COVID-19 might reshape public demands for social protection in settings where welfare institutions are not highly developed or inclusive.

The historical trajectories of welfare state development in Southeast Asia are distinctive as well. In most Western countries, the rise of welfare states was closely linked to the growing influence of trade unions, Leftist parties, and the broader labour movement, often occurring alongside processes of democratisation and industrialisation (Korpi, 2018). Welfare state expansion was driven by demands for social protection and redistribution, advocated by well-organised actors and coalitions committed to social welfare (Baldwin, 1990). However, the countries of Southeast Asia, as late developers, experienced rapid economic growth in the postcolonial period, much of which was overseen by authoritarian regimes. In countries such as Indonesia, Malaysia, the Philippines, Singapore, and Thailand, 'developmentalist' authoritarian regimes prioritised economic growth and political stability over social welfare expansion, co-opting or suppressing labour movements to avoid social unrest.

The repression of the political Left was also a common feature of these regimes. During the Malayan Emergency between 1948 and 1960, a communist insurgency was crushed in peninsular Malaysia. The Indonesian Communist Party (PKI) was brutally dismantled in the mid-1960s during the early Suharto dictatorship. In Thailand, various military-backed governments repressed communist and other Leftist political movements from the 1950s to the 1970s. Singapore's PAP first purged its ranks of the Leftist Barisan Sosialis in the early 1960s and continued to repress Left-wing groups such as the Workers' Party over subsequent decades. In the Philippines, Ferdinand E. Marcos' martial law rule (1972–1986) involved not just a prolonged anti-insurgency campaign against the communist New People's Army but also a crackdown on labour groups and legal Leftist political activists and parties. The repression of the Left in these Southeast Asian countries often led to their 'political demise' and along with it the loss of 'their agendas of radical social, economic and political transformation' (Hewison and Rodan, 2011: 20). This repressive political climate weakened the forces typically associated with the expansion of welfare states – namely, progressive political parties, independent labour unions, and welfare-focused civil society groups. As a result, Southeast Asia's welfare states have developed in a conservative, minimalist fashion.

At the same time, despite these broad regional similarities, Southeast Asia exhibits significant intraregional heterogeneity in sociodemographic factors and political institutions. The region today encompasses a diverse range of political regimes, from authoritarian states such as Cambodia and Vietnam to electoral democracies like Indonesia, the Philippines and Timor-Leste as well as hybrid regimes like Malaysia and Singapore. Countries such as Singapore and Vietnam have demonstrated long-term political stability, while others, including Malaysia, Myanmar, and Thailand, have been marked by political instability, military coups, and shifting alliances. Electoral democracies like Indonesia, the Philippines, and Thailand have been backsliding in recent years (Mietzner, 2021; Thompson, 2023; Kongkirati, 2024). Of the two electoral authoritarian regimes in the region, Singapore has recently experienced further democratic regression (Tan and Preece, 2024). The other, Malaysia, underwent a partial democratic transition after the opposition surprisingly won the 2018 elections, but began backsliding again in 2020, though this was partially reversed in the aftermath of the 2022 elections (Weiss,

2022). These variations in regime type are significant because they influence how governments respond to crises like the COVID-19 pandemic, shape welfare policies, and determine the degree to which citizens can express and influence their policy preferences.

For this study, we selected five cases on which to focus – Indonesia, Malaysia, the Philippines, Singapore, and Thailand – each of which maintains at least some degree of democracy or electoral participation.[1] All of these countries have experienced democratic backsliding over the last decade and Singapore remains an electoral authoritarian regime. But all five countries' regimes remain at least somewhat responsive to public opinion and face electoral challenges, often to a significant degree. Thus, because regimes in these five countries still have an important electoral component and at least some democratic participation, it might be expected that if pressures arise from civil society demanding policy change, regimes will prove responsive. More specifically, we believe it is a reasonable assumption that during the critical juncture created by a pandemic, a decisive shift in public opinion will increase pressure on the regimes for policy change. Whether – or to what extent – this pressure will lead to change is discussed at length in this book.

In addition, the social and ideological structures in Southeast Asian regimes are further shaped by distinctive historical and cultural contexts. In Malaysia, ethnic identity is a major determinant of political preferences, while in Indonesia, political competition is strongly influenced by debates over the role of Islam in public life (Fossati, 2022). Although Singapore is officially a multi-ethnic nation, a major social cleavage has existed been between an ethnic Chinese, English-educated faction long dominant in the PAP and a perennially marginalised Chinese-educated working class (James, 2022). In Thailand, political divisions are more fluid due to volatile alliances, but regional divides and the contentious role of the monarchy remain central fault-lines (Ferrara, 2015). Despite a substantial Muslim minority, the most enduring social cleavage in Philippine politics has been between different, predominantly Christian, ethnolinguistically defined regions (Dulay et al, 2022). Amid these varying cleavages, economic redistribution has rarely been a prominent political issue in the region, largely due to the historical weakness of Left-wing movements and labour unions discussed earlier.

Southeast Asian countries also exhibit significant variation in the levels of political legitimacy, an important indicator for which is the level of trust their populations place in national governments. According to the data we have collected (Figure 1.1), Singapore stands out with the highest level of trust in its government, with 53.5 per cent of the population reporting a high level of trust in national government (8 or higher on a scale ranging from 1 to 10), followed closely by Indonesia. In contrast, Malaysia and the Philippines show lower levels of trust, and Thailand has the lowest level, with just 24.8 per cent of the population having a high degree of trust in the national government.

This variation might be attributed to a mix of recent developments and longer-term factors. In Singapore and Indonesia, for instance, high trust levels may result from the government's consistent performance in ensuring economic development and stability, while the lower levels observed in Malaysia and Thailand could be due to issues such as political and social polarisation resulting in instability, and, in the case of Thailand, the persistence of authoritarian government despite social demands for deep political reform. These differences in government legitimacy are important for our study of COVID-19-induced attitudinal and institutional change, as public trust influences how citizens respond to crisis management measures, including possible changes in social policy. In countries where trust is high, governments may be more successful in ensuring policy compliance. Citizens may be more likely to have confidence in the government's ability to expand the scope of existing social policy programmes.

TAKING STOCK OF THE PANDEMIC IN SOUTHEAST ASIA

Figure 1.1: Institutional trust in five Southeast Asian countries

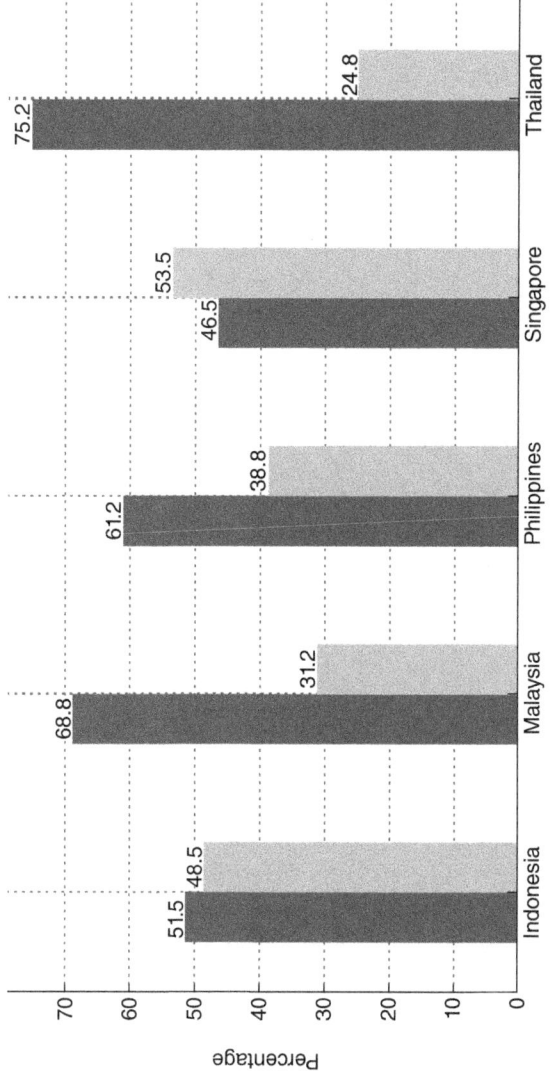

Note: A score of 8 or higher on a trust scale ranging from 1 to 10 reflects 'high trust'.

The five countries we study also exhibit significant variation in their levels of socioeconomic development. Singapore stands out as the most advanced economy in the region, with high levels of gross domestic product (GDP) per capita (USD 61,491 in actual US dollars in 2020 according to the Asian Development Bank's key indicators), a well-developed infrastructure, and a highly urbanised population. Malaysia (USD 10,399 per capita) and Thailand (USD 7,199) follow as upper middle-income countries with well-diversified economies and advanced infrastructure in major cities. Indonesia (USD 3,920) and the Philippines (USD 3,326) remain middle-income countries where, despite continuing economic progress, poverty and inequality are still substantial issues and a large share of the population is only informally employed. Apart from Singapore, all countries also feature stark divides between rural and urban populations in terms of access to services, infrastructure, and economic opportunities, with urban areas generally benefiting from higher levels of development and modernisation, while rural regions often experience poverty, underemployment, and limited access to healthcare and education. These shape each country's capacity to implement social policies and respond to crises, and they may therefore be critical for understanding the uneven impact of crises such as COVID-19 on both public attitudes and institutional change across Southeast Asia.

The Southeast Asian countries we study, then, not only allow us to address a gap in the literature on non-Western responses to COVID-19, but also differ significantly among themselves as well as when compared with Western cases. This high level of heterogeneity provides an ideal laboratory within which to study the dynamics of public opinion and policy change in developing societies during times of crisis.

Diseases, policies, and legacies

Southeast Asia has long been a crossroads of human interactions. In pre-colonial times, the spice trade brought goods and people from Northeast Asia through Southeast Asia and beyond, fostering the creation of permanent trade routes and settlements. People bought and traded animals and opened up new ecosystems to urbanisation, combining multiple wellsprings for the spread of infectious diseases. Later, the establishment of colonial settlements provided a new set of opportunities for the spread of diseases between Europe and Southeast Asia, as the global reach of the European powers created new links between the region and other parts of the world.

As these transmission links were being forged, states and institutions sought ways to stop the diseases from spreading. Tagliacozzo (2014: 49, 52) has shown how the annual pilgrimages from ports such as Singapore or Batavia (present-day Jakarta) to Mecca became transmission routes for the spread of cholera, smallpox, malaria, dengue fever, and amoebic dysentery. In response, West Asian states created a new array of testing, quarantine, and treatment facilities in and around Mecca as well as offshore. They did so as an early recognition that the close proximity of so many persons was likely to exacerbate the spread of these diseases and also that the returning pilgrims would be carriers of the diseases back to their home societies.

In more recent times, regional health cooperation began with the first Association of Southeast Asian Nations (ASEAN) Health Ministers Meeting, held in 1979, and a follow-up meeting in July 1980 when the regional health architecture started to be shaped. At the end of the second meeting, the ministers had identified eight core areas for further regional cooperation: primary healthcare; disease control; health planning, management and information system; nutrition; health manpower development; environmental and occupational health; pharmaceuticals, biologicals and traditional medicine; and mental health. These areas were to be addressed via a new regional health architecture set up within the overarching structure of ASEAN.

Despite this list of areas for further collaboration, the institutional development of regional health did not proceed quickly. The third ministerial meeting, focused on health and nutrition, was only held four years later. By the time of the fourth ministerial meeting in 1991, diseases – specifically the looming threat posed by HIV/AIDS – created sufficient impetus for further institutional evolution in this area. Reflecting the seriousness of the AIDS threat, the Indonesian health minister suggested a new information exchange framework between ASEAN members. This framework assisted members in sharing information and experiences on disease control, especially with regard to policy formulation and the implementation of control programmes. However, this collaboration did not result in any homogenisation of policy approaches but remained purely technical, with each country choosing its own pathway to engaging with HIV/AIDS (or other diseases).

Nonetheless, by the end of the 20th century, a regional health architecture had begun to emerge in Southeast Asia. It was a structure that, although still state-centric, was starting to incorporate private sector actors, civil society organisations, and professional networks. In doing so, the health sector – on the surface – displayed a more inclusive set of norms than other parts of the ASEAN organisation. However, while a wider array of actors may have joined the regional health policy fora, it remained a state-dominated process – one largely driven by regime norms and development agendas rather than the prioritisation of health issues.

As a result, the emergence of severe acute respiratory syndrome (SARS) in southern China in November 2003 presented a major challenge to regional health institutions and social systems even though only six of the states were affected, with only three of these (Singapore, Vietnam, and Thailand) suffering double-digit deaths. In terms of the institutional responses, it is noteworthy that Southeast Asia was ill-equipped to respond to the threat of SARS – at either the regional or state levels – in a timely manner. The special meetings of ASEAN,

ASEAN–China, and ASEAN+3 were only convened in April 2003, when the crisis was already receding in most affected countries. This delay reflected not only the priority accorded to the outbreak relative to other policy concerns in the member states, but also the challenges of health cooperation in a region where geopolitical concerns still dominated institutional agendas. These delays and challenges suggest that health issues were seen as an outcome of policy processes by states rather than a driver of those same processes. This, in turn, reflects the highly heterogeneous nature of Southeast Asian approaches to health and disease issues, a characteristic that was to be seen again with the outbreak of COVID-19.

Furthermore, while it was recognised that both the medical community and civil society needed to be brought into the policy response processes, the incorporation of those groups was hampered due to the domestic political environments in individual countries, as was the case with responses to HIV/AIDS. This was a pattern that would be followed with the later HPAI, H5N1, and H1N1 outbreaks (Thomas, 2006), where the political and historical legacies of earlier outbreaks, rather than the threat posed by the disease itself, shaped the disease response. Indeed, during these later outbreaks, the additional resources and capacities offered by the medical and civil societies was only unevenly drawn on by regional states due to domestic policy/political constraints (Pongcharoensuk et al, 2012) and the limited or short-run impact on policy agendas. Due to these regime-centric responses, major disease outbreaks in Southeast Asia since the turn of the century have had far higher social and economic costs than could have otherwise been the case with an integrated, collective response.

COVID-19 in Southeast Asia

The experiences from disease outbreaks before the COVID-19 pandemic defined the policy environment into which COVID-19 emerged. Unlike in earlier outbreaks, which only affected subsets of countries in the region, the economic development of China since the turn of the century and its sociopolitical enmeshment with Southeast Asia meant that all regional states were on the front line of the COVID-19 pandemic. This, in turn, meant that all states would be exposed to the pandemic, with the only questions being when and how severe would the impact be.

As with most other regions, Southeast Asia experienced three major waves of the pandemic: the initial wave in early 2020, the Delta variant wave in 2021, and the Omicron variant wave in 2022. While variation in reporting standards means that a final death toll will never be precisely known, ASEAN statistics show the significant impact the virus had on regional countries (Table 1.1). Despite the high death toll, however, COVID-19 caused fewer fatalities than many other causes of death. For example, in 2017, non-communicable diseases accounted for an estimated 8.5 million deaths in ASEAN countries (approximately 62 per cent of regional deaths), a figure that has been trending upwards (Castillo-Carandang

Table 1.1: COVID-19 cases in Southeast Asia (as of 5 March 2023)

Country	Total confirmed cases	Total deaths
Brunei	279,661	225
Cambodia	138,720	3,056
Indonesia	6,739,067	160,948
Laos	218,023	758
Malaysia	5,045,192	36,967
Myanmar	633,955	19,490
Philippines	4,077,904	66,210
Singapore	2,234,996	1,722
Thailand	4,728,304	33,924
Viet Nam	11,527,037	43,186

Source: Data from ASEAN BioDiaspora Virtual Center (2023)

et al, 2020: 803). Thus, the outbreak was more of a challenge in terms of the stresses it placed on the regional healthcare systems (Jones, 2023: 145) and the disruptions from the negative externalities caused in other areas of sociopolitical and socioeconomic behaviour.

In terms of policies, the pandemic did not disrupt the political life of states and institutions in Southeast Asia as much as it did in other regions around the world. Mostly, this lack of disruption was a reflection of the centralisation of authority in all of these states, even in those with democratic characteristics. This was accompanied by a shrinking civic space that fostered anti-government challenges or discourses in all countries. As Maude (2020) observes:

> Expanded executive powers to fight the pandemic are being misused to stifle political opposition, close down space for civil society and attack free media. In some 'partly free' Southeast Asian nations, military-led responses to the pandemic have been ineffective, led to human rights abuses and have boosted military influence at the expense of civilian administrations.

Across the region, all states implemented short-term measures to protect poorer households and small businesses. These measures were paralleled by other responses, such as the provision of enhanced social insurance, in addition to workplace protections and adaptive behaviours such as teleworking. Nevertheless, the majority of COVID-19 welfarist responses were limited to six months or less. While some early analyses suggested that the outcomes from COVID-19-related policy responses could lead to regional states 'reinventing' their social welfare systems (Mok et al, 2021: 8) to develop along similar lines, the short-term nature of many of the anti-pandemic measures meant that the pre-existing policy structures continued largely unaffected.

The institutional stickiness of welfare structures reflects the fact that in Southeast Asia there is a clear link between ensuring ongoing economic productivity and welfare support. As Yuda et al (2022: 312) conclude, this means that during COVID-19, 'such attempt[s] [became] particularly important in ensuring economic stability at the required levels to prevent capital outflow and excessive unemployment'. Within such an ideological construct, the survival of a regime becomes predicated on its ability to deliver economic goods and benefits to its population. This, in turn, creates an overriding institutional rationale for the regional governments to return to normal operations (or a close approximation thereof) as soon as possible after a crisis. Indeed, as Ku and Yeh (2022: 166) conclude, 'the COVID-19 pandemic is sure to have long-term impacts on social policy, leading to a resurgence of big government'.

That said, the economic impact of the pandemic was severe across Southeast Asia, which did present a challenge to regional governments' ability to successfully manage the crisis. IMF data show that the first year of the pandemic was particularly hard, with all countries recording marked year-on-year declines in GDP (Fraser, 2022), while in the second year most countries returned to positive growth. It was only by 2023 that regional states mostly returned to GDP growth levels comparable to 2019. However, at the time of writing, the severe impact on the more marginalised, lower socioeconomic groups within these countries means that their economic well-being is yet to recover to pre-pandemic levels.

The economic downturn forced regional governments to adopt short-term economic stimulus packages to keep their economies on track. While partially successful insofar as the economies still functioned and were able to engage in global trade, the global reality of the pandemic meant that the fiscal stimulus packages were limited in scope and impact. This led to shortfalls in support and a corresponding shrinking in the provision of public goods and the domestic private sectors. As a result, there was a sharp rise in people across the region who fell into extreme poverty (5.4 million) with corresponding rises in unemployment and economic distress (ASEAN, 2020). These pressures meant that the regional states were under pressure to return to growth as soon as possible.

In choosing between an early reopening of their economies and prioritising infection control, Southeast Asian governments generally chose the former option. In November 2021, Thailand became the first Southeast Asian state to open its borders. This created a domino effect, with most states dropping border restrictions for inbound travel in the first half of the following year. With the Omicron variant still in circulation, it would take until 2023 for the economies to stabilise and begin to grow again, but after three years Southeast Asia began slowly – and unevenly – returning to a 'new normal'.

This new normal was not just a result of institutional and economic policies but also a reflection of the levels of acceptance of the types of novel personal behaviours needed to mitigate the impact of the virus within regional societies. As An and Tang (2020: 791) observe, '[to] be effective, any policy instrument requires public cooperation and voluntary compliance. Policy instruments that infringe on individual freedom are more feasible and sustainable in East Asian culture that emphasises collectivism'. Supporting evidence for this can be found in Aspinall et al (2021: 34), where respondents across a range of Southeast Asian states supported the suspension of freedoms and the introduction of emergency laws in addition to the militarisation of the pandemic in order to deal with the threats posed by it. When the data were disaggregated by county, only the Philippines and Indonesia were opposed to stronger government interventions at the expense of individual rights and freedoms (Aspinall et al, 2021: 32).

Hence, going into the pandemic, there was a foundation for social cooperation and compliance when it came to new anti-pandemic policies and practices – one that was built on the legacies of successful responses to past outbreaks as well as overlapping levels of positive trust in government performance, interpersonal relations, and the medical community. As shown in later chapters, this combination of factors provided a strong basis for government actions that, in turn, allowed regional states to orient their responses towards the maintenance of the status quo rather than being forced to develop novel policy pathways and practices.

Book structure

In the remainder of this volume, Chapter 2 discusses key theoretical tools for interpreting the survey and qualitative institutional data presented in this study. After a discussion of the relevant concepts of historical institutionalism, and of critical juncture analysis especially, the chapter focuses on factors that mediate change at both the individual attitudinal and institutional levels. At the individual level, we draw on theories of political psychology (Albarracín and Shavitt, 2018) to explain the conditions under which individuals may adjust their policy beliefs in response to significant events like the COVID-19 pandemic. The mediating factors we analyse include trust in government, partisan and ideological orientations, perceptions of crisis management, affective responses linked to pandemic exposure, and a sense of attachment to national identity. At the institutional level, we borrow from theories of institutional change (Mahoney and Thelen, 2010) and critical junctures (Sorenson, 2023) to explore how selected institutional factors – including state ideology, populism, clientelism, and legitimacy – shape the extent and direction of institutional responses to crises. By bridging these complementary frameworks, the chapter highlights the interplay between individual-level processes and institutional environments in shaping pandemic responses.

Chapter 3 presents empirical findings from an original survey conducted in five Southeast Asian countries, examining how the COVID-19 pandemic has influenced public preferences regarding social policy. Respondents were asked to reflect on whether their attitudes towards key social policies, including social insurance, government involvement in healthcare, and economic redistribution, had shifted because of the pandemic. The results indicate that COVID-19 is widely perceived as a transformative event, with significant attitudinal shifts towards greater support for more generous social policy provisions. The chapter analyses variation in these changes across different social groups and national contexts, highlighting how factors such as economic status, political ideology, and trust in government affect individuals' policy preferences. A regression analysis is also included to identify the key drivers of attitudinal change, offering insights into the factors that promote or hinder shifts in public opinion.

Chapter 4 examines the political dynamics and policy responses to COVID-19 in the five case countries, comparing initial responses to the pandemic and subsequent policy performance. The chapter highlights substantial variation across countries in terms of crisis management and policy implementation. In Singapore, for example, the persistence of a technocratic anti-welfarist ideology limited the scope of policy change, while in Indonesia and the Philippines, a combination of populism and clientelism hindered the development of comprehensive social policy reforms. In Malaysia and Thailand, political instability and shifting alliances similarly constrained meaningful policy transformation. Despite these differences, the chapter documents a convergence in the policy measures ultimately adopted across the region, with all five countries employing a similar set of responses, such as stimulus packages and healthcare expansions. The chapter concludes by assessing whether these developments indicate a long-term expansion of state institutions and welfare provisions, or if the changes remain primarily reactive and short-term in nature.

The final chapter synthesises the findings from the preceding chapters and reflects on their broader implications for the ongoing debate on social policy in non-Western political settings (Aspalter, 2006). This chapter aims to integrate the empirical results from Chapters 3 and 4 within the theoretical framework outlined in Chapter 2, offering a comprehensive analysis of how both public opinion has been shaped by and how political institutions have responded to the pandemic in Southeast Asia. This synthesis of the findings of the study and discussion of their implications is followed by a comparative analysis of developments in Southeast Asia and other regions in which we assess the specificity of Southeast Asia and comment on the prospects for the emergence of more comprehensive and inclusive welfare states in the region. The chapter also explores long-term prospects for social policy development in Southeast Asia, considering whether the pandemic has opened a window for more permanent welfare state expansion or whether institutional and political constraints are likely to limit sustained change.

TWO

Theorising possibilities of change

A novel pandemic cannot, by definition, be anticipated. There are few measures a country can enact to directly protect itself in advance. Instead, policy makers and social actors default to responses shaped by previous outbreaks: social distancing, physical isolation, quarantines, closure of gathering sites, and the wearing of masks and other protective garments. Under such circumstances, pandemics create a series of disruptions between the way the state and society functioned in the pre-outbreak period and what occurs during the pandemic and how the country regains control in the post-pandemic period. We draw on historical institutionalism in framing how these disruptions may lead to policy and behavioural responses. In this chapter, we review the core ideas contained in this theory before offering an account of how it can be applied to better understand the institutional and attitudinal change in the context of the COVID-19 pandemic in Southeast Asia.

Historical institutionalism

At its core, historical institutionalism concerns the study of institutions as formalised sets of processes and actors, and how these change over time. It is useful in building a model from 'empirical puzzles that emerge from observed events or comparisons' (Thelen, 1999: 373).

In seeking to explain how policy choices lead to different institutional policies and social formations, historical institutionalism scholars frequently draw on path dependency analysis to identify critical junctures – a period during which decisions are made that may forge a new institutional arrangement. As Ma (2007: 64) explains, path dependence means that 'once a social process has started, it will produce its own law of inertia through which the cost of adhering to the original direction of change will decline, whereas the cost of switching away will rise'. During a critical juncture period, however, the underlying institutional and social conditions provide a window of opportunity for those switching costs to fall, allowing new policy and societal pathways to be explored. However, this is not an automatic outcome but rather the result of competition between interested policy constituencies.

The issue of sequencing also becomes important in identifying the time frame within which the institutions and related processes catalyse to form a critical juncture. As Sorenson (2023: 932) notes, 'it is assumed that history matters, and that actors can, in certain situations, have an impact on outcomes, that contests over public policies can lead to contingent choices that have lasting impacts'. However, the time frame within which these contests and impacts take place is somewhat ambiguous. Capoccia and Keleman (2007: 348) define 'critical junctures as relatively short periods of time during which there is a substantially heightened probability that agents' choices will affect the outcome of interest'. However, the actual period of time is 'brief relative to the duration of the path-dependent process that it instigates' (Capoccia and Keleman, 2007: 348). In other words, for short-run disease outbreaks (severe acute respiratory syndrome – SARS – in 2003, for example) a critical juncture can be easily identified. For diseases that span longer periods (such as COVID-19), a longer temporal backdrop or a greater impact needs to be identified.

While historical institutionalism focuses primarily on macro-level change, a parallel micro-level process of attitudinal and behavioural change may take place among ordinary citizens. Such psychological processes can unfold through various channels, both cognitive and affective (Bish and Michie, 2010). First, a crisis almost instantly increases perceptions of risk, urgency, and the salience of a specific policy area as the emergency becomes ubiquitous in mass media and other communication settings. As a result, citizens may develop new priorities and adopt new behaviours. Second, crises bring about an information overload that exposes individuals to new knowledge (Rathore and Farooq, 2020). In the case of a pandemic, citizens may learn new things about the specific health threat they are facing, features of the healthcare systems, social inequalities, and government performance, which could then alter their conception of and preferences about public policy. Finally, emotional and affective responses may play a critical role in shaping attitudinal and behavioural shifts during crises (Kim and Niederdeppe, 2013). Heightened stress, fear, and perceptions of vulnerability may make citizens more likely to support radical actions or accept restrictions that would otherwise be contentious. In the next chapter, we examine attitudinal change through an original survey which shows how views of social policy were affected by the pandemic in the five Southeast Asian countries analysed in this book.

During crises, then, critical junctures may emerge in which state institutions and ordinary citizens undergo processes of disruption at various levels. By unpacking the different stages of the process, it is possible to analyse the possibilities of rapid change in times of crisis. Doing so also affords an opportunity to better understand how and why, in this case, the states of Southeast Asia responded to the pandemic, and what this means for the future development of the welfare state in the region.

Modelling pandemic responses

Sorenson (2023: 934) proposes a five-stage model explaining institutional change within any period marked by disruptive changes in policy and social behaviours. The first stage is the existence of antecedent conditions, against which the scale of the changes can subsequently be measured. The second stage is the existence of conditions permissive to change. Even in the event of a crisis – caused by a pandemic or something else – it would still be possible for a state not to change if the institutional and social conditions were not permissive to adaptation. The mutability of this structure is, in turn, determined by compliance costs and benefits tied to domestic and international factors (such as treaties, norms, loans, and other commitments; Simmons, 2000). Hence, there has to be both a causally linked set of precedents as well as a structure that is open to change. The third stage is that of the critical juncture, which is defined by conditions able to produce change in institutional policies and social behaviours. Both the permissive and productive conditions are essential elements in any critical juncture. However, the response to a threat and the emergence of a critical juncture is not a linear model. The allocation of resources away from status quo recipients to respond to the crisis creates reactions and counter-reactions in both state institutions and society. This is the fourth stage. The final stage – the outcome of the crisis – emerges when the situation stabilises to a sufficient degree that the dominance of the productive conditions is substantially reduced.

Before a critical juncture can emerge, there must be conditions permissive to the formation of the juncture. Permissive in this sense can be seen both positively and negatively. On the one hand, the presence of permissive conditions may indicate a high degree of flexibility in the system. This would indicate a greater institutional and social capacity able to adapt rapidly to the challenges presented by the pandemic. Alternatively, a fragile system – one overwhelmed by the pandemic – would need to enact rapid change in order to survive. In such a scenario, a 'cleavage or crisis that develops from the antecedent conditions provides the permissive conditions to open the critical juncture and create possibilities for change' (Thaler, 2022: 4). A third possibility, however, is that a system facing acute instability may become 'overwhelmed' during a crisis, leading to a 'near miss' in which policy change that might have been expected during a political crisis does not occur (Capoccia, 2015). This is part of a more general phenomenon in which 'the political forces in favour of institutional change narrowly lose their struggle to forces favouring stability – in other words, cases in which the political struggle over the choice of different institutional options during a phase of uncertainty and institutional fluidity results in *re-equilibration* rather than change' (Capoccia, 2015: 166, emphasis added). In Chapter 4, we argue this possibility of a 'negative' outcome of a critical juncture – in which policy change was possible but did not occur – was particularly likely in systems, such as in Southeast Asia, where elites before, during, and after the pandemic played a dominant role in state–society relations while civil society was often weakened and opposition parties were marginalised or co-opted.

Such negative outcomes are instances of counterfactual cases – examples where the conditionality for a critical juncture is met but where the new pathway does not form. Capoccia and Kelemen (2007: 352) propose that in such cases a recalibration of the regime 'or the restoration of the pre-critical juncture status quo' might be plausible outcomes. In other words, the critical juncture can still form but there is no substantive deviation from past institutional practices and/ or attitudes. Such outcomes can be expected when – as is the case in most Southeast Asia states – there is a lack of effective opposition in either the political or social realms or when there are elite strategies that can weaken potential resistance, or a combination of both. In such cases, elites and their ideologically aligned social representatives have already weakened opposing forces or, if they remain potentially powerful, undermine their ability to make effective demands during the critical juncture. Either possibility essentially freezes the institutional and social structures, making it harder for alternate policy approaches to gain traction.

During a critical juncture, the capacities of both state and societal actors are placed under strain as the event – in this case, the COVID-19 pandemic – challenges the ability of the actors to continue pursuing pre-juncture policies. That said, as Rinscheid et al (2020) conclude, exactly how these actors respond to the challenge remains somewhat opaque and undertheorised. Their study suggests that change from the pre-juncture period would only occur if those 'preexisting conditions push central agents to deviate from the status quo and incite a collective re-orientation of beliefs' (Rinscheid et al, 2020: 671). Drawing on Shim (2024: 101), it can be suggested such a deviation is more plausible when either elites (and the governing institutions) become fragmented in their approach to the issue or social actors are more united than the regime in addressing the crisis (or when both conditions are present). Once that deviation occurs, the antecedent and permissive conditions that were present prior to the critical juncture are joined with the productive conditions that respond to the institutional and social pressures for change.

Productive conditions are those that 'can be defined as the aspects of a critical juncture that shape the initial outcomes that diverge across cases' (Soifer, 2012: 1575). If permissive conditions provide the opportunity for change, productive conditions enable the change to occur. These types of conditions include factors that 'structure the sets of actors, change mechanisms, and choices of institutional change during a critical juncture' (Sorenson, 2023: 935). That said, the initiation of institutional and social change creates further disruption. In particular, as the focus of the state moves towards addressing the challenge that created the critical juncture, a reallocation of resources and policy development is required. Given the extent of government and society responses that are needed to combat a pandemic, it is not surprising that this reallocation would be resisted by deprived sectors. The longer resources are reallocated the greater the decline in permissive conditionality by institutional and societal actors.

However, a critical juncture cannot be sustained indefinitely as the attention of actors and the needs of the state change over time. The longer the critical juncture the greater the likelihood of institutional and social resistance building up as sectors that have lost or been denied resources seek to change their circumstances. While there can be counter-reactions to such policy resistance, as other issues inevitably demand the attention of policy makers or impinge on social awareness, attention as well as resources will inevitably shift and the permissive and/ or productive conditions will come to an end. As shown in Chapter 4, the potential for this period of change to endure diminishes and, eventually, ends when the conditions that support it are no longer permissible. In this respect, even when the productive conditions were present without concomitant permissive conditions, the juncture closed.

In the case of the COVID-19 pandemic, almost all states around the world sought a return to normal before the virus had ceased to be a threat. Again, the productive forces (in terms of increased morbidity and mortality arising from the virus) were still present but the permissive conditions attenuated and ended as counter-reactions to pandemic exceptionalism continued. In every case, this was due to institutional or social pressures that acted as a brake on prioritising ongoing pandemic measures over other policy issues. As a result, the critical juncture closed as the reactive sequence was no longer dominated by the permissive conditions that enabled change to occur in the first place. Instead, the reactions against pandemic policies and behaviours dominated the policy and social spaces and forced a return to pre-crisis institutional modes. In this study, these pressures arose from non-health sectors that sought relief from the restrictions imposed by the pandemic.

In doing so, the states in Southeast Asia (and beyond) drew on antecedent conditions informed by their current developmental needs as well as the impact from previous outbreaks to close the critical juncture ahead of the disease being eradicated. This set of decisions provides this book with an analytical backdrop against which social policy changes during and after the pandemic can be assessed.

Drivers of change

When analysing responses to critical junctures, it is essential to consider the role of a range of macro- and micro-level variables that may function as antecedent, permissive, or productive conditions and thus explain variation in institutional and attitudinal change across countries and individuals. At the micro level, key factors include social and institutional trust, ideological and partisan orientations, sociodemographic factors such as age and education, and emotional and affective responses like fear or solidarity. These individual-level variables influence public attitudes, behaviours, and compliance with crisis management measures, making them crucial in shaping societal responses to critical junctures. At the macro level, factors such as regime type, state capacity, legitimacy, citizen–politician linkages, and dominant ideologies (including technocracy and populism) may significantly influence institutional decision making and crisis response strategies. These factors shape the political landscape, determining how inclusive or centralised responses are and how resources are allocated. Taken together, these aspects are at the heart of institutional and social responses to any critical juncture, forming two levels of mutually reinforcing factors that enable and shape a state's response.

Individual-level factors

At the individual level, we can find substantial heterogeneity in responses to a crisis such as a pandemic. While some individuals may change their behaviours significantly – for example, by severely limiting their social interactions to reduce infection risk – others may be reluctant to do so and may refuse to comply with government prescriptions. Some may take the crisis as an opportunity to learn and to update some of their views on important social and political issues, and others will fail to do so. Several studies have analysed such diverging patterns of individual-level attitudinal and behavioural change and tried to identify factors that may account for them.

A crucial variable emerging from this literature is trust, understood in its various forms such as interpersonal trust and institutional trust (Campos-Castillo et al, 2016). Trust is a pivotal driver of behavioural responses during a crisis, as research on COVID-19 has convincingly demonstrated (Ayalon, 2021). The adoption of behaviours such as wearing face masks, accepting vaccinations, washing hands/using hand sanitiser, and social distancing implicitly relies on an individual's inherent acceptance or trust in the efficacy of those measures. More broadly, support for government policies that enforce prosocial behaviours – vaccine campaigns, border controls, and quarantines – also require trust in the legitimacy, competence, and effectiveness of state institutions. Institutional trust is therefore a necessary element of any state's ability to develop and enact policies (Han et al, 2023).

Trust plays a crucial role not only in shaping behavioural responses but also in influencing attitudinal shifts during crises, such as a pandemic. It acts as a key mediator in how individuals assess the credibility of the information they receive and conceptualise the potential policy options and their implications (Agley et al, 2021). This is particularly relevant during crises that ignite debates over expanding the role of government, as previous research has shown that trust is related to support for larger government (Rudolph and Evans, 2005). In a pandemic, proposals for greater government involvement in healthcare or the expansion of social safety nets may be received more favourably by individuals who trust the government's capacity to manage such initiatives effectively. Trust therefore functions as a filter through which individuals evaluate the necessity and efficacy of institutional responses, making it a critical factor in determining whether a crisis leads to lasting attitudinal change.

In addition to trust, other factors that have been shown to be significant drivers of attitudinal and behavioural change include variables of political or ideological nature, such as partisanship, evaluations of government performance, and broader ideological orientations. For instance, research on COVID-19 has revealed substantial partisan differences in cognitive, affective, and behavioural responses, especially in polarised societies such as the United States (Gadarian et al, 2021). Partisanship also shapes how individuals evaluate policy performance, which is closely linked to their perceptions of a government's trustworthiness and the legitimacy of proposed policies (Altiparmakis et al, 2021). Moreover, broader political–ideological divides influence attitudes towards government intervention, with individuals who identify as conservative often being less supportive of an expanded governmental role in crisis management (Ruisch et al, 2021; Dochow-Sondershaus, 2022). In short, ideological, political, and partisan predispositions are powerful sources of variation in attitudinal responses to a crisis, influencing not only acceptance of specific policies but also broader debates about the expansion of government powers and potential threats to individual freedoms during such periods.

Affective factors are also important in shaping an individual's response to a crisis. In a pandemic, emotions such as anxiety, fear of infection or death, and feelings of vulnerability can be powerful drivers of attitudinal and behavioural change (Coifman et al, 2021). These emotions heighten an individual's sense of urgency and perceived risk, leading to greater compliance with health directives and a stronger desire for protective policies. Related to this, one of the most important factors influencing attitudinal and behavioural responses is direct exposure to the crisis itself. Individuals with a higher degree of exposure to the adverse effects of the crisis may be more likely to experience feelings of anxiety and undergo shifts in their opinions and behaviours.

Finally, another affective factor that has received considerable attention in existing studies is attachment to national identity. Crises tend to be exceptional moments that impact large segments of the population, and they may foster a sense of solidarity and heightened awareness of belonging to a national community. For example, studies of COVID-19 have documented 'rally round the flag' effects, where national crises lead to increased support for incumbent leaders as citizens rally behind them in the face of an external threat (Hegewald and Schraff, 2024).

Institutional-level factors

In democratic countries, regular elections and changes in power and authority between political parties provide a key mechanism to translate changing social preferences into policy change. When such regularised methods fail, protests and other forms of resistance may emerge. Lam and Chan (2015) found that authoritarian regimes magnify the disruption of the critical juncture, suggesting that the return to the 'new normal' may be more problematic for those forms of governance than for democratic systems facing similar threats. This possible disjuncture between state and societal actors would put such regimes under intense pressure, as society would demand changes in responses to acute threat while the state would strive to maintain the status quo. However, a reverse case – of a democratic challenge – can also be envisaged, where the demands from society cause the state to respond in ways that diverge from its original policy intentions. During both the critical juncture and the post-outbreak periods, the regime structures the varied state and societal dynamics that shape crisis response. These structures, in turn, determine the capacity of the regime to govern and to respond to challenges.

In this study, capacity refers not only to the absolute capacity of the regime but the capacity of the state as perceived *relative* to the challenges posed by the pandemic. Southeast Asia has a wide variation in state capacities, from countries with deep capacities to deal with systemic shocks (such as Singapore) to those with low capacity (such as Laos or Myanmar). In terms of a critical juncture formed by the pandemic, however, the utility of this capacity needs to be weighed against the perceptional challenges posed by the crisis. In countries that were sensitised to emergent infectious diseases, those perceptions were centred on the regimes' capacity to respond in a timely manner. Where states were not sensitised to disease outbreaks or where the pandemic itself was not perceived as being an existential challenge relative to other threats (such as developmental shortcomings), regime capacity was less challenged by the pandemic. In other words, capacity and perceptions are mutually intertwined. Where states had higher response capacities or had other policy priorities that were framed as holding equal or greater weight to the pandemic, it is suggested that there was a lower institutional need to undertake long-lasting social welfare responses. Where there was a lower capacity or an absence of competing policy priorities, there would be higher institutional pressure for greater social welfare responses.

An active civil society and an effective political opposition able to act as agents of change in the formation of a more inclusive welfare state system are other factors that influence capacity and perceptions. Numerous studies highlight the critical role of Leftist political parties, demonstrating that social policies tend to be more generous and inclusive where such parties have gained significant strength (Allan and Scruggs, 2004; Kriesi et al, 2006). Similarly, trade unions and working-class mobilisation have historically played a pivotal role in advocating for redistributive policies (Korpi, 2006). However, in contexts where economic redistribution is not a salient political issue or where working-class mobilisation is weak, the dynamics become more fluid and complex. In these settings, other actors, such as non-governmental organisations, grassroots movements, or even technocratic elites, can emerge as key agents of change. For example, NGOs often mobilise resources and expertise to address gaps in welfare provision (Banks and Humle, 2012), while grassroots movements can amplify marginalised voices, demanding reforms and proposing innovation during moments of crisis (Farid, 2019). These options underscore the importance of context-specific dynamics and the interplay of diverse agents in shaping the trajectory of welfare state development.

Ideological factors may also be crucial in explaining state responses to disruptive crises. In the context of Southeast Asia, two ideologies in particular have been influential. The first is technocracy: a self-referential political arrangement based on a claim to exclusive meritocracy meant to insulate itself from public discussion and critique (Habermas, 2015). Viewed through a neoliberal lens, social welfare measures are only justifiable in helping the worst off in society or to address unforeseeable contingencies. Such measures must not interfere with the overriding goal of preserving stable markets and, after exceptional emergency measures, a return to 'normal', non-interventionist governance (de Visser and Straughan, 2021). Countries with regimes in which technocracy is a dominant ideology are therefore more likely to quickly discontinue 'emergency' social welfare measures in the name of restoring fiscal stability and to reinforce their ideological opposition to 'welfarism'.

The second key ideology is populism, which is often depicted as the opposite of technocracy. Populism is commonly understood as a 'thin', anti-pluralist ideology or political style pitting the 'pure people' against a corrupt and duplicitous elite undertaking policies inimical to the common interest (Moffit, 2016). Several studies have examined the relationship between populism and welfare state development, demonstrating that this relationship is complex and context dependent

(Kaltwasser and Zanotti, 2021). On the one hand, populism is linked to economic grievances, suggesting that it could be conceptualised as a reaction to economic deprivation and increasing inequality. On the other hand, because populism lacks a coherent economic doctrine, its social policy agenda is largely shaped by the host ideology of the movement. Left-wing populism has typically advocated for an expansion of welfare provisions, emphasising redistribution and social rights (Font et al, 2021), whereas Right-wing populism frequently promotes welfare chauvinism, endorsing social benefits for the 'native' or 'deserving' population while restricting access for immigrants and marginalised groups (Ketola and Nordensvard, 2018). Ultimately, the relationship between populism and the welfare state is contingent on national context, and it often reflects a tension between inclusionary and exclusionary approaches to social protection.

Political clientelism, or the allocation of benefits by politicians in exchange for political support (Kitschelt, 2000), is also a powerful determinant of social policy outcomes. While clientelistic linkages may provide some short-term material gains for low-income groups, as they facilitate a limited degree of redistribution and accountability, they are inherently exclusionary and particularistic. As a result, clientelism can weaken a country's capacity to adopt more inclusive and universal social policies by prioritising selective, contingent benefits over broad-based welfare programmes. This dynamic undermines programmatic policy making, as political actors become more focused on maintaining patronage networks than on institutionalising long-term social protection measures or other types of policy reform (Cruz and Keefer, 2015). When clientelism dominates resource allocation, it functions as a distinct mode of interest intermediation, shaping both political competition and economic governance in ways that entrench dependency rather than structural reform (Trantidis, 2016).

Aside from the institutional, ideological, and political factors discussed earlier, regime legitimacy is also crucial in understanding the effectiveness of a state's response to a crisis (Christensen et al, 2016). Political legitimacy is understood here as the regime's capability to meet popular expectations based on beliefs of what constitutes justifiable rule. High levels of popular support during an unprecedented pandemic can enhance a regime's capacities for dealing with the pandemic, potentially improving performance. This is likely to bolster regime stability but also potentially lower pressure for long-term policy change. A low level of popular support for a government attempting to cope with a global pandemic is likely to lead to an unvirtuous cycle in which civil society protests contribute to further policy incoherence by governments preoccupied with political survival. Mistrust engendered by a government's lack of popular support is likely to affect its governance abilities (Reid et al, 2023). This issue becomes particularly acute at times of crisis such as during the outbreak of a pandemic, when citizens would normally look to government for guidance and to provide assistance to those most affected.

The process of change

While key macro- and micro-level factors that shape the policy implications of critical junctures can be identified, the mechanisms through which they generate change remain contested. Critical junctures create windows of opportunity for significant policy shifts, but such changes are neither automatic nor uniform, and the process through which crises may or may not translate into policy change is complex, unpredictable, and deeply political. It is useful to highlight four key mechanisms that help explain how permissive and productive conditions for change emerge: coalition formation, the role of policy entrepreneurs, shifts in public opinion, and policy diffusion. These mechanisms provide a basis for understanding how critical junctures can lead to lasting policy transformations or why they fail to do so.

First, coalition formation allows diverse actors, such as political parties, civil society groups, and interest organisations, to align around common goals and push for reform, leveraging their collective influence to overcome resistance. Emmenegger's (2021) study of agency advanced the argument that institutional change requires social coalitions which have sufficient strength to demand change. Coalitions can gain agency by increasing their bargaining power during periods where reforms are encouraged by elites and institutions. They do so by providing an opportunity to 'appropriate a structured institutional context which favours certain strategies over others and they do so by way of strategies that they formulate or intuitively adopt' (Hay and Wincott, 1998: 955). Although this implies the presence of a feedback mechanism between public opinion, social activism, and policy change during a crisis, the impact that such coalitions have on institutional practices is largely dependent on the nature of the regime. While these processes can occur during critical junctures, it is not automatic that the outcome will lead to a new pathway forming. Such coalitions can, equally, stabilise the institutions by defending them against attacks from challenger coalitions.

Second, policy entrepreneurs play a vital role by navigating institutional complexities, framing issues, and seizing moments of instability to form coalitions and advocate for innovative solutions and change. This does, however, depend on the extent to which the crisis that precipitates the instability is perceived as requiring de novo policy innovation. As discussed earlier, where the perception is that the crisis exceeds the institutional capacity or jeopardises other critical areas of policy implementation, policy entrepreneurs are able to advocate for innovation. Conversely, where these perceptions are absent or only weakly held, there is far less scope for change, even within a critical juncture. As Feitelson et al (2022: 11) conclude, 'policy learning differs as a function of the specific experience and conditions in each country'. Variation due to regime type and capacity becomes the norm rather than a homogenised institutional response to crises.

Third, shifts in public opinion in response to a crisis can amplify demands for change and mobilise support for reform agendas or, conversely, bolster resistance to transformation. This is where the perception of the crisis – in this case, the COVID-19 pandemic – becomes a key determining factor. In states that were previously sensitised to infectious disease outbreaks, the greater awareness of the potential threat posed by COVID-19 helped to bolster support for reforms. As Ru et al (2021) found, societal responses to COVID-19 were far more proactive in SARS-exposed states than elsewhere. Even within states, Chen et al (2020) observed that cities previously exposed to SARS had higher levels of public awareness and policy responsiveness than counterparts without that social memory. The issue that then arises is to what extent such opinions are able to gain traction with policy makers within and beyond the critical juncture. This is considered in the following chapters.

For these reasons, we would suggest that the sociopolitical nature of the regime needs to be factored in to, or considered alongside, the constraint of collective action. Across the spectrum of regimes that exist globally and, for the purposes of this study, regionally in Southeast Asia, there are the more liberal systems that allowed social perspectives to influence institutional responses to policy issues both before and during the pandemic. But there are also the more illiberal or authoritarian systems that were only minimally responsive to such perspectives and pressures in the same periods. Extending from the work of Thelen (1999) and Emmenegger (2021), we would suggest that the ability of social forces to have the necessary agency to bring about change is based on their capacity to influence the reproduction and feedback mechanisms of the institutions that govern them. In the following chapters, these social perceptions of the pandemic and accompanying policy responses as well as the institutional reaction to those perceptions and the pandemic will be examined.

Conclusion

A pandemic disrupts the status quo, creating a clear divide between what happened before the outbreak and what happened during and after the pandemic. Analysing the state response to such a challenge has been the focus of multiple theoretical schools. As this study has a strong institutionalist policy aspect, we have drawn on historical institutionalism as the main explanatory framework. In essence, this model proposes a multistage process through which states move as they seek to address the threat: moving from the pre-threat legacy antecedents to the mobilisation of permissive and productive conditions to the outcomes of the critical juncture. Within each of these stages there are different factors and elements that need to be present if the process is to yield the desired resolution of the threat. While the literature frequently presents this type of model as a linear process, as discussed earlier, challenges with regards to the sequencing of policies and behaviours, the emergence of alternate junctures, and the rise of counter-narratives render state responses far more fluid and chaotic in nature.

One possibility discussed in existing research is that a state with relatively strong institutional capacity and a regime oriented towards enhancing social capacity may be more likely to respond to a crisis such as the COVID-19 pandemic by implementing major policy change. Conversely, a regime operating in a fragile state may also pursue rapid transformation, not from a position of strength but as a strategy of survival in the face of overwhelming pressures. However, it is equally plausible that a regime confronting acute instability may choose to implement only minimal adjustments – just enough to preserve the status quo and avoid deeper reforms. This may result in what Capoccia (2015) describes as a 'near miss' – a scenario in which significant policy change appears possible but ultimately does not materialise as forces favouring institutional continuity prevail over those advocating transformation. In

Chapter 4, we further examine how this 'negative' outcome of a critical juncture – where change was conceivable but unrealised – was particularly likely in the political systems of the Southeast Asian countries we analyse, where elite dominance in state–society relations remained largely intact before, during, and after the pandemic.

THREE

Attitudinal and behavioural change

In this chapter, we analyse how ordinary citizens in Indonesia, Malaysia, the Philippines, Singapore, and Thailand perceive their changes in opinions and behaviours resulting from the pandemic. We start by introducing key features of our data and discussing some measurement issues as well as some descriptive statistics. Then, we leverage our survey data to investigate if, and to what extent, Southeast Asians perceive the pandemic as a transformative event that changed how they think about important social policy issues and the possible need for more inclusive and comprehensive social welfare policies. We analyse variation in attitudinal change across social groups and countries. Next, we shift the focus to identifying drivers of attitudinal change through regression analysis, and we perform a similar analysis of behavioural change. We give special attention to factors such as risk exposure, institutional trust, and partisan and ideological orientations. We summarise the results in the concluding section.

Measures and attitudes

Our study is based on five original web-based surveys conducted in Indonesia, Malaysia, the Philippines, Singapore, and Thailand. These surveys were implemented using panels recruited by an international survey company, and participants were incentivised through small material rewards. The surveys were administered through personal smartphones, laptops, or similar devices in multiple languages, including English, Malay, simplified Chinese, Tagalog, Indonesian, and Thai, depending on the country. Data collection occurred simultaneously across all countries over several weeks in May to early June 2023. Each country's sample size was 1,200 respondents. In choosing to collect data through web-based surveys and recruit respondents without random selection, an important limitation of our study is that the samples are not fully representative of the populations they are drawn from. Nevertheless, as reported in the table in the appendix on the sociodemographic composition of the five samples, the samples do show a substantial level of diversity across a range of sociodemographic variables. While the breakdown does not faithfully mirror the population of each country, it ensures us that the samples are diverse enough to analyse the role of a range of sociodemographic backgrounds in shaping attitudinal change and that individuals of all walks of life are included in our study. The non-representative nature of the sample, then, while warranting caution when making estimates about the populations of interest, does not diminish our ability to investigate key relationships between variables or test theoretical mechanisms.

The main outcomes that we were interested in measuring are attitudinal and behavioural changes resulting from the COVID-19 pandemic. Ideally, measuring such changes would involve panel data so that the outcomes of interest could be measured before and after the supposedly transformative event. As this was not possible, we relied on questions that directly ask our respondents about changes they perceived, which presents some methodological challenges (Jaspers et al, 2009). One primary issue is the potential for recall bias, where respondents may not accurately remember or may misrepresent their past attitudes and behaviours. Additionally, social desirability bias can influence respondents to provide answers they believe are more socially acceptable rather than reflecting their true beliefs or actions. To mitigate these problems, we followed recommended practices and designed questions that can help reduce ambiguity and improve accuracy of recall by being clear, parsimonious, and specific in referencing the pandemic (Hipp et al, 2020). Regardless of such methodological issues, however, we believe that studying perceptions of attitudinal and behavioural change is valuable even if they do not perfectly align with actual change. These perceptions can reveal underlying cognitive and emotional processes that drive how individuals interpret and respond to new information or experiences, and they may influence behaviour and decision making.

Our key question asking about change in social policy preferences included a battery of statements in randomised order, introduced by the following prompt:

> The COVID-19 pandemic has had a significant impact on societies and economies worldwide. As a result, public attitudes on various issues related to the welfare state and health policy may have shifted. For each of policies listed below, please indicate if the COVID-19 pandemic has changed your opinions. Has the pandemic made you more supportive or less supportive of these policies, or has it made no difference?

In the list following this prompt, respondents were asked to report the extent to which the pandemic has made them supportive – that is, much less supportive, less supportive, no difference, more supportive, or much more supportive – of policies that that increase the role of government in: healthcare, insuring people against accidents or sickness, protecting people from job loss (that is, unemployment benefits), protecting people from falling into poverty, improving workers' education and skills, improving childcare services, introducing a basic income for all citizens, aiming to reduce inequality, increasing the role of government in the economy, and redistributing economic wealth from the rich to the poor. These statements measure attitudinal change in a broad range of areas, including some that are closely related to health policy but many others that address the social vulnerabilities and inequalities that the pandemic so dramatically exposed. Moreover, we asked if the COVID-19 crisis had changed their support for international cooperation on healthcare policy, since this was a salient political issue during the pandemic, especially in the early stages.

As for measuring behavioural change, we designed a series of questions that ask respondents if at the time of the survey – after the acute phase of the pandemic was over – they had changed various health-related behaviours. Specifically, we asked if they were more likely than before the pandemic to observe social distancing precautions, wash their hands, wear a mask in public, and avoid large gatherings of people.

In addition to measuring public perceptions on how people shifted their views on social policy and their health behaviour as a result of the pandemic, an important goal of our analysis was to identify factors associated with such change. To this end, we designed a series of questions measuring demographic characteristics of the respondents as well as various theoretically relevant factors.

First, the survey incorporated several demographic variables to capture the socioeconomic background of respondents. In addition to gender, age was measured in years. The median age was 41, indicating that older respondents were under-represented, as is typically the case for web-based surveys. Education was recorded as a dummy variable, where 0 signifies no college education and 1 indicates possession of a college degree. Notably, our sample was substantially better educated than the general populations in the countries where the survey took place, with 59 per cent holding college degrees, 23 per cent with only a high school education and 18 per cent with lower levels of education. Income was measured on a four-level scale reflecting financial stability: 1 indicates struggling to make ends meet, 2 indicates the ability to cover basic needs, 3 indicates the capacity to save a small amount each month, and 4 indicates financial security. The sample was very diverse in this regard. More than one quarter indicated they struggle to make ends meet, while only 12 per cent reported they feel financially secure.

Second, the survey examined respondents' experiences with the COVID-19 pandemic, recognising that the high degree of heterogeneity in exposure levels can significantly affect attitudinal and behavioural change in response to the pandemic. An ordinal variable was constructed based on four binary questions asking if respondents had been infected with COVID-19 and if they had lost a friend or family member, lost access to healthcare, or lost a job as a result of the pandemic. Overall, 23 per cent of the sample answered negatively to all four questions, suggesting that many were relatively sheltered from the pandemic's direct impacts. Conversely, 61 per cent scored either 1 or 2 on this index, indicating some degree of exposure. Additionally, we measured respondents' feelings of vulnerability to disease risk through a question encompassing concerns about various infectious diseases – not just COVID-19 but also malaria, tuberculosis, dengue fever, and bird flu – with responses ranging from 1 (not worried at all) to 7 (extremely worried). The indicator variable built as the mean of all these responses had an average score of 4.72 across the five samples, suggesting a fairly high level of concern among respondents.

Third, institutional trust and evaluations of institutional performance during the COVID-19 crisis were critical variables in the survey, as previously discussed. Trust in public institutions was measured by asking respondents how much they trust the national government, the local government, the army, the media, and medical and scientific experts. These responses were combined into an index ranging from 1 (no trust at all) to 10 (trust completely). As discussed in Chapter 1, trust levels vary significantly across both individuals and countries, with national government trust being notably high in Singapore and Indonesia, much lower in Thailand, and intermediate in Malaysia and the Philippines. Perceptions of COVID-19 performance were measured by asking respondents to agree or disagree with statements comparing their country's pandemic response and recovery to that of other nations. Specifically, the items stated that the country did better than other countries in dealing with the pandemic and is recovering better than other countries. Responses ranged from 1 (strongly disagree) to 5 (strongly agree). Average values indicated more critical assessments in the Philippines (3.15) and Thailand (3.24), and more positive evaluations in Singapore (3.92), with Malaysia (3.53) and Indonesia (3.72) in between.

Fourth, political attitudes and social identities were also examined, given their potential influence on the dependent variable and other theoretically relevant factors. Partisanship was measured by support for the incumbent president or prime minister – a relevant indicator in Southeast Asia, where political party systems can be fluid. Support for the incumbent varied widely, from 24 per cent in Thailand to 66 per cent in Indonesia. Ideology, particularly support for economic redistribution, was measured by agreement with the statement 'The government should provide more assistance to the poor, even if it means raising taxes', with responses ranging from 1 (strongly disagree) to 5 (strongly agree). The mean score of 3.26 suggests a moderate level of support for redistribution. Finally, attachment to national identities was assessed using an ordinal variable measuring feelings of closeness to the nation, with 0 indicating not very close or not close at all, 1 indicating somewhat close, and 2 indicating very close. Most respondents reported feeling close to their nation, with 47 per cent being somewhat close and 30 per cent very close. This highlights the potential impact of national identity on 'rally round the flag' effects during the pandemic.

Table 3.1 reports descriptive statistics for all these variables, and the next sections provide a closer look at how the two

Table 3.1: Descriptive statistics for the variables in the survey

Variable	Values	Frequency	Per cent/mean	Cum/SD	Min	Max
Age	–	6,000	41.20	14.31	18	96
Gender	Male	2,988	49.80	49.80		
	Female	3,012	50.20	100		
	Total	6,000	100			
College education	No	2,471	41.18	41.18		
	Yes	3,529	58.82	100		
	Total	6,000	100			
Income	I struggle	1,631	27.18	27.18		
	I cover my basic needs	2,037	33.95	61.13		
	I am able to save	1,619	26.98	88.12		
	I am financially secure	713	11.88	100		
	Total	6,000	100			
Exposure to COVID-19	0	1,437	23.95	23.95		
	1	2,207	36.78	60.73		
	2	1,460	24.33	85.07		
	3	658	10.97	96.03		

Table 3.1: Descriptive statistics for the variables in the survey (continued)

Variable	Values	Frequency	Per cent/ mean	Cum/ SD	Min	Max
	4	238	3.97	100		
	Total	6,000	100			
Worried about disease risk	–	6,000	4.72	1.59	1	7
Trust in public institutions	–	6,000	6.61	1.84	1	10
Evaluation of COVID-19 performance	–	6,000	3.51	1	1	5
Support for the president	No	2,838	47.30	47.30		
	Yes	3,162	52.70	100		
	Total	6,000	100			
Ideology (support for redistribution)	–	6,000	3.26	1.22	1	5
National Attachment	Not close	1,379	22.98	22.98		
	Somewhat close	2,792	46.53	69.52		
	Very close	1,829	30.48	100		
	Total	6,000	100			

Notes: cum: cumulative %; min: minimum value; max: maximum value; SD: standard deviation

key outcomes we measured – namely, attitudinal change and behavioural change – varied across individuals, social groups, and samples.

Who has changed their attitudes about social policy?

In Chapter 2, we discussed various institutional, historical, and individual-level factors that shape how ordinary citizens and political elites may respond to crises and change. In this section, we leverage our original survey data to identify micro-level factors associated with attitudes about social policy and to measure their effect on attitudinal change. Before doing that, however, an analysis of how perceptions of attitudinal change vary across policy area, social group, and country is in order. This analysis allows us to address a key question on the legacy of COVID-19 in Southeast Asia: to what extent have citizens 'learned' from the pandemic and updated their social policy preferences?

Based on the mean of the responses to the nine questions on social policy preferences, outlined in the previous section, we built an index of perceived attitudinal change as a synthetic indicator. This measure ranged from 1 for respondents who consistently stated that they had become much less supportive of the various policy measures to 5 for those who had become much more supportive of the measures. Across the five samples, the mean value of this index was 3.76 – a value that sits between 3, which denotes no change in attitudes, and 4, which indicates that an individual has become more supportive of social policies as a result of the pandemic. This value suggests that most respondents expressed the general sentiment that COVID-19 has indeed changed their mind on some important social policy issues. At the same, however, the fact that the average was below 4 indicates that such perceived change may be contingent on the specific policy being considered.

To facilitate data analysis and interpretation, we recoded this indicator as a binary variable, assuming a value of 1 for those scoring 4 or higher, who could be seen has having become more supportive of more comprehensive social policies on most issues. To be sure, this is a rather high standard to set, as some respondents may have become more supportive of certain important social policy initiatives even if they did not satisfy this criterion. However, this approach ensured a more rigorous assessment of attitudinal change by reducing the risk of overestimating the extent of support for broad-based social policy reforms. It thus provided a clear, intuitive benchmark to compare attitudes across the five samples. This synthetic indicator indeed varied significantly across countries in the survey data we collected. In most cases, only a minority of respondents scored 4 or higher on the index, which again suggests that the pandemic led to a substantial degree of attitudinal change, but only in some areas and for some citizens. Singapore was the country with the lowest recorded share (36 per cent) of respondents categorised as having become substantially more supportive of social policy programmes because of the pandemic, while Indonesia had the highest share (52 per cent), and the remaining three countries fell in between these two cases (42 per cent in Malaysia and 45 per cent in both the Philippines and Thailand). While our data alone are not sufficient to explain this divergence, the intriguing contrast between Indonesia and Singapore is evidence that context-specific factors play an important role in shaping learning and changing preferences as a result of disruptive events. Perhaps this difference could be attributed to the specific trajectory of welfare state development in Singapore, a country that has been especially conservative and reluctant to adopt high-expenditure social programmes, even compared with other Southeast Asian countries (Hwang, 2020).

To what extent, then, do perceived changes in social policy preferences vary across policy areas? As mentioned earlier, the nine statements were designed to measure variation in policy preferences in areas that are closely related to the disruptions brought about by the pandemic as well as in others that, while

Table 3.2: Perceived change in support for various social policies

	Percentage who are supportive
Policies that increase the role of government in healthcare	67.6
Policies that insure people against accidents or sickness	62.5
Policies that protect people from job loss (that is, unemployment benefits)	64.5
Policies that protect people from poverty	62.9
Policies that improve workers' education and skills	65.4
Policies that improve childcare services	60.1
Policies that introduce a basic income for all citizens	61.9
Policies aimed at reducing inequality	57.8
Policies that increase the role of government in the economy	58.0
Policies to redistribute economic wealth from the rich to the poor	56.0

important for welfare state development, are not as closely linked to the COVID-19 experience. Table 3.2 reports results for the pooled data, showing a full overview of support for the various policies. Specifically, the figures shown are the share of respondents who reported that they were somewhat more supportive or much more supportive of the policies because of the COVID-19 pandemic. The results clearly show a high degree of perceived attitudinal change among our respondents, as for each policy, a majority of respondents reported increased support. There is thus little doubt that many Southeast Asian citizens believed they had changed their social policy beliefs as a result of the pandemic. At the same time, however, the table shows substantial differences across policy areas, as the share of respondents reporting increased support ranges from a high of 67.6 per cent for a larger role of government in healthcare to a low of 56 per cent for increased economic redistributions. Again, this suggests that despite widespread perceptions of increased support for various social policy programmes, support for more inclusive policies may vary significantly across policy areas, social groups, and countries, especially for more controversial policies to reduce inequality.

To investigate variation between these two groups of policies (that is, policies closely related to COVID-19 and broader welfare state development policies) more systematically, we built two additional binary indicators – the first based on statements about policies closely related to the pandemic and the second on broader policies.[1] Figure 3.1 shows the difference between these two sets of policies across the five countries. Not surprisingly, the patterns of variation across countries were quite similar to the ones discussed in the previous paragraph, with Singapore and Malaysia showing overall lower levels of perceived attitudinal change than other cases, followed by Thailand and the Philippines with somewhat higher increases in support for COVID-19-related and welfare state policies, and Indonesians being the case with the highest level of reported attitudinal change in both categories. It is also interesting to note that respondents in all countries were more likely to report having become more supportive for the more specific set of COVID-19-related policies than for broader welfare policy initiatives. This suggests that learning and preference updating are more likely for policies that are perceived as being more closely related to an emergency than to broader welfare policies.

To further investigate variation in attitudinal change across countries, we asked whether the pandemic has made respondents more supportive of international cooperation to address healthcare issues. Especially in the early stages of the pandemic, the interconnectedness of national healthcare systems was exposed as collective action and resource-sharing across borders were sorely needed to manage the outbreak. This crisis may thus have led many respondents to better

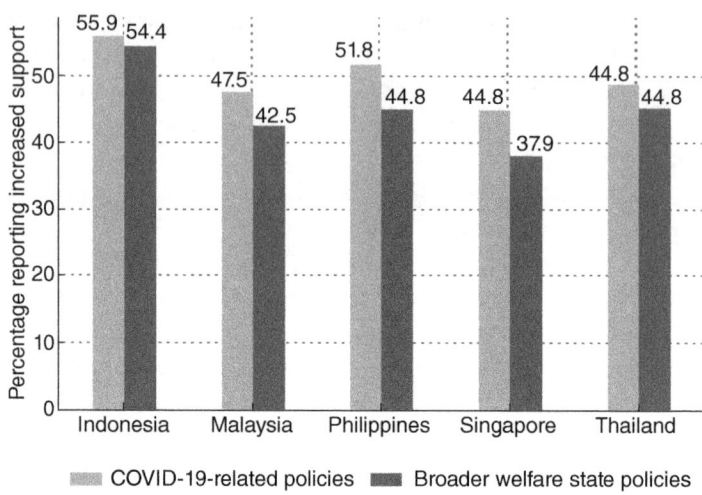

Figure 3.1: Increased support for social policies in five countries

appreciate the importance of international cooperation in addressing global health challenges. The distribution of responses to this question, reported in Figure 3.2, contrasts with the previous chart in that, first, a decisive majority of respondents reported having become more supportive or much more supportive of international cooperation and, second, variation across countries was more limited. To be sure, the statement we designed was rather general, as it did not indicate specific types of international cooperation or the costs that might have been associated with such cooperation. Nevertheless, these data indicate a high level of awareness among Southeast Asian publics of the importance of the international dimension of the pandemic and possibly a belief that international cooperation is at least as important as domestic policies in mitigating the risk and managing the consequences of such transboundary crises.

Socioeconomic factors such as education, income, gender, and age may play an important role in shaping attitudinal changes towards social policy, as they could influence how

ATTITUDINAL AND BEHAVIOURAL CHANGE

Figure 3.2: Change in support for international cooperation in healthcare

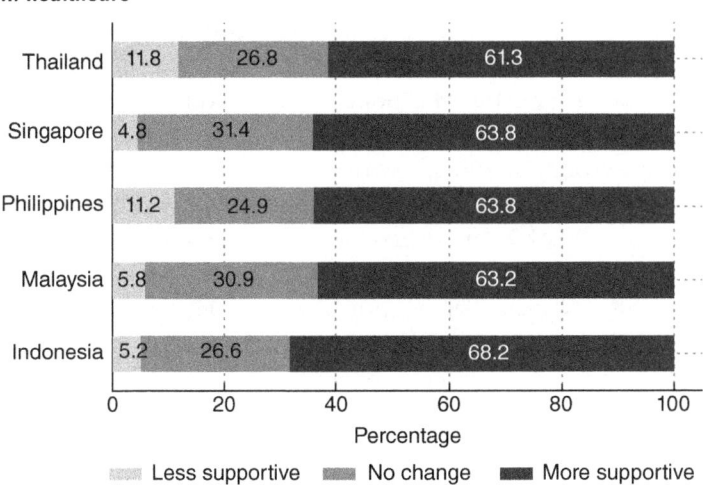

individuals perceive and support government interventions. Education, for example, is typically associated with stronger cognitive skills and greater exposure to policy discourse and critical thinking. As attitudinal change is a learning process, we could expect that those with higher education levels may be more likely to have become more supportive of broader welfare policies. Income could also play a role, as individuals with lower economic security may have been more exposed to pandemic disruptions, potentially increasing their support for social safety nets. Existing research has also documented gender differences in responses to the pandemic, both in terms of emotional responses (Laufer and Shechory Bitton, 2021) and attitudes and behaviours (Galasso et al, 2020). As women have been generally more anxious about epidemiological and social implications of the pandemic, they may be more likely to have become supportive of welfare state expansion. As for age, older individuals have been shown to perceive lower levels of various types of risks associated with the pandemic (Bruine de Bruin, 2021), which might imply higher rates of attitudinal change among younger individuals.

The data displayed in the four panels reported in Figure 3.3 show some variation in support for COVID-19-related policies and broader welfare state policies across education, income, and gender, but barely any variation by age group. In terms of education, respondents with no college education showed substantially lower support than college-educated individuals for both COVID-19 policies (46 per cent compared with 41 per cent) and broader welfare policies (53 per cent compared with 48 per cent), supporting the expectation that higher education is associated with greater ability to learn and update policy preferences, though not confirming the hypothesis that those who are less well off will be more supportive of increased social welfare provision. Variation across income groups was less pronounced than for education, and this is contrary to the expectations outlined in the previous paragraph, since those struggling financially were less supportive of both policy types than those who are financially secure.[2] This difference could be attributed to differences in educational attainment between these two groups and to feelings of lower trust and political agency among those who are worse off. Trust in the national government was substantially lower among low-income individuals (33 per cent reported high trust in government, according to the indicator in Figure 1.1) than among the financially secure (51 per cent). Gender differences were contrary to expectations based on the existing literature too, with men showing somewhat higher, not lower, support than women for COVID-19 policies (52 per cent compared with 48 per cent) and broader policies (47 per cent compared with 42 per cent). This is a surprising finding, given that women in our sample were only marginally less educated than men, and that they reported overall higher levels of anxiety about risk of infection and pandemic implications as well as higher levels of exposure to the disruptions of COVID-19 than men. As for age, support for both COVID-19 policies and welfare

ATTITUDINAL AND BEHAVIOURAL CHANGE

Figure 3.3: Change in support for social policy among different sociodemographic groups

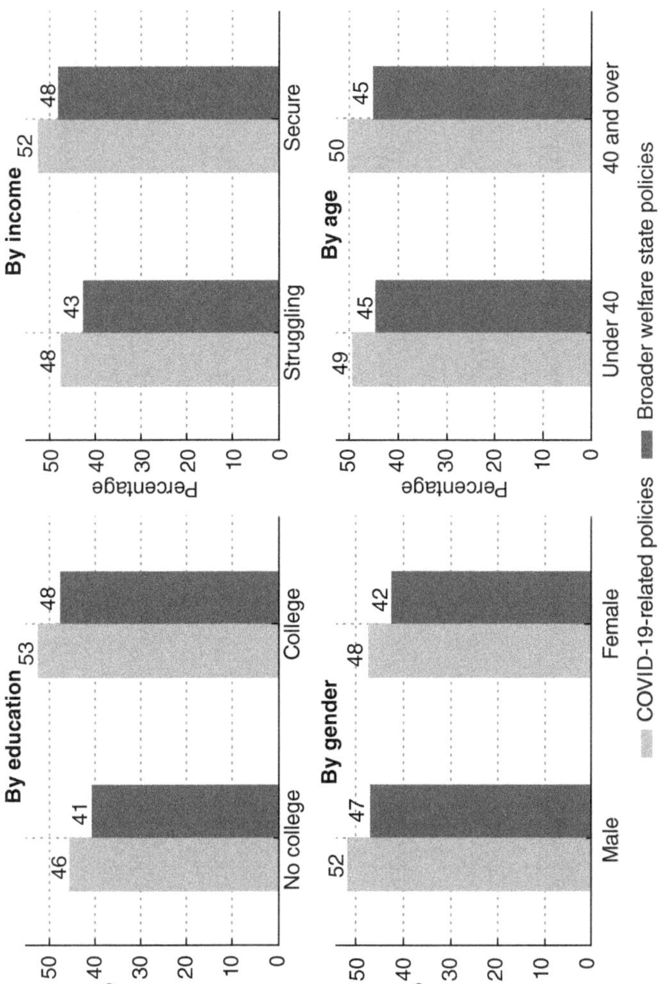

By education
- No college: COVID-19-related policies 46, Broader welfare state policies 41
- College: COVID-19-related policies 53, Broader welfare state policies 48

By income
- Struggling: COVID-19-related policies 48, Broader welfare state policies 43
- Secure: COVID-19-related policies 52, Broader welfare state policies 48

By gender
- Male: COVID-19-related policies 52, Broader welfare state policies 47
- Female: COVID-19-related policies 48, Broader welfare state policies 42

By age
- Under 40: COVID-19-related policies 49, Broader welfare state policies 45
- 40 and over: COVID-19-related policies 50, Broader welfare state policies 45

Table 3.3: Determinants of attitudinal change in five countries

Variables	(1) Indonesia	(2) Malaysia	(3) Philippines	(4) Singapore	(5) Thailand
Exposure to COVID-19	0.198*** (0.0577)	0.0301 (0.0630)	0.133*** (0.0587)	−0.0334 (0.0736)	0.251*** (0.0575)
Trust in public institutions	0.197*** (0.0483)	0.152*** (0.0454)	0.204*** (0.0418)	0.218*** (0.0538)	0.0803*** (0.0403)
Evaluation of COVID-19 performance	0.303*** (0.0814)	0.223*** (0.0891)	0.114 (0.0669)	0.294*** (0.0999)	0.0824 (0.0774)
Support for the president = 1	0.213 (0.145)	0.351*** (0.133)	−0.188 (0.133)	−0.0878 (0.159)	−0.103 (0.162)
Worried about disease risk	0.146*** (0.0437)	0.172*** (0.0472)	0.123*** (0.0428)	0.135*** (0.0456)	0.132*** (0.0388)
Ideology (support for redistribution)	0.314*** (0.0538)	0.108*** (0.0550)	0.153*** (0.0498)	0.301*** (0.0608)	0.265*** (0.0486)
National attachment	0.0872 (0.0926)	0.318*** (0.105)	0.463*** (0.0932)	0.347*** (0.114)	0.318*** (0.0905)
Age	−0.00112 (0.00523)	−0.00475 (0.00461)	−0.00326 (0.00489)	−0.0109*** (0.00481)	−0.00481 (0.00527)

Table 3.3: Determinants of attitudinal change in five countries (continued)

Variables	(1) Indonesia	(2) Malaysia	(3) Philippines	(4) Singapore	(5) Thailand
Gender = 2, Female	−0.319*** (0.132)	−0.193 (0.129)	−0.145 (0.127)	−0.328*** (0.135)	0.0611 (0.125)
College education = 1	0.182 (0.139)	0.216 (0.128)	0.354*** (0.141)	0.165 (0.138)	0.336*** (0.138)
Income	0.0631 (0.0639)	−0.0625 (0.0670)	0.0226 (0.0745)	−0.0665 (0.0748)	0.105 (0.0665)
Constant	−4.746*** (0.468)	−3.587*** (0.458)	−3.713*** (0.428)	−4.495*** (0.569)	−3.250*** (0.391)
Observations	1,200	1,200	1,200	1,200	1,200
Log-likelihood	−722.3	−748.3	−754.3	−710.0	−761.1

Notes: Standard errors are given in parentheses. *** $p < 0.05$.

policies was virtually identical between respondents younger than 40 and those older than 40.

The data therefore indicate that, except for education, sociodemographic factors were generally not a very powerful driver of variation in attitudinal change, and theoretical expectations derived from existing studies were often not supported.[3] These inconclusive results, however, should not be interpreted as suggesting that no significant difference in attitudinal change exists across social groups as defined by sociodemographic covariates, because significant factors such as institutional trust, emotional responses to the pandemic, evaluation of government performance, or pandemic exposure may well be correlated with an individual's social background. These findings therefore highlight the need to look beyond demographic factors and consider more specific indicators of pandemic experience and responses as well as broader political and ideological orientations. In the next sections, we perform regression analysis to investigate the role of these factors, first for attitudinal change and then for behavioural change.

Analysing the drivers of attitudinal change

With this picture in mind of variation across countries and policy areas, we now shift the focus of the analysis to the individual level. Table 3.3 reports logistic estimation results for the five countries in the sample for models in which increased support for social policies (that is, the binary indicator described earlier, based on the average of the nine survey questions) is a function of various experiential, ideational, political, and sociodemographic factors. While substantial variation across countries was observed for some factors, other factors appear to have had an important effect on attitudinal change in most settings.

Starting with experiences with the pandemic, exposure to COVID-19 was significantly linked with attitudinal change in three of the five survey countries – namely, Indonesia, the

Philippines, and Thailand. In these countries, individuals with higher levels of exposure were more likely to have become more supportive of social policy expansion. Interestingly, this positive effect of pandemic exposure on support for more generous social policies was not observed in Singapore and Malaysia, possibly due to lower inequalities in COVID-19 exposure in these countries. Overall, however, the effect of exposure to the pandemic can be substantial. For example, in the Philippines, the predicted probability of increased support for social policies was about 41 per cent for an individual with little exposure to the pandemic, but this increased to 53 per cent for a respondent who lost loved ones, their job, and access to healthcare during the pandemic. Concerns about vulnerability to infection also positively impacted attitudinal change, and their effect was remarkably consistent across countries. This shows that in all of the counties surveyed, individuals who were more concerned about the risks of infection were more likely to report that they had become more supportive of various social policies.

These results point to the importance of individual experiences with the pandemic in shaping cognitive responses to it. While COVID-19 forcefully disrupted the lives of most people, it is essential to remember that heterogeneity in exposure to the pandemic was substantial – the pandemic had a much heavier toll on some than it did on others, and emotional responses varied significantly across individuals as well. Those who were more exposed to the disruption, and sometimes to the most tragic consequences of the pandemic, were more likely to have changed their mind about what the government could, and should, do to mitigate related risks.

Institutional trust and evaluations of institutional performance during the COVID-19 crisis are also important factors for attitudinal change. Institutional trust, measured through the index described in the previous section, was significantly and positively associated with attitudinal change in all countries, although the magnitude was lower in the case of Thailand, the country with the lowest aggregate levels of trust in government. In this respect, our surveys build on existing research to provide further evidence of the importance of the role of trust in shaping various aspects of cognitive and behavioural responses to the pandemic. They show that people with higher levels of trust in government and related institutions are more likely to change their preferences and increase their support for comprehensive social policy programmes. For example, in Indonesia, for an individual with high levels of trust in government (index value of 8), the predicted probability of becoming more supportive of social policies was 57 per cent, but this figure dropped to only 44 per cent for a respondent with a lower level of trust (index value of 5). Evaluations of institutional performance were similarly positively linked with perceived attitudinal change, although in this case the results were only statistically significant for the cases of Indonesia, Malaysia, and Singapore.

These findings remind us of the importance of the views of institutions in shaping cognitive responses to the pandemic. When conceptualising an important event like a pandemic and evaluating its implications, strengthening institutions and expanding the role of government may increasingly be perceived as crucial. Yet, the desirability of increased social spending or government reach may be contingent on a person's (or a society's) view of how legitimate and trustworthy government institutions are in the first place. Our results indeed suggest that citizens with lower levels of trust in government institutions, or less satisfaction with how they handled the pandemic crisis, are less receptive of the idea that trusting institutions with new tasks and endowing them with more resources could be a desirable or effective option to manage future crises.

Existing research also suggests that political orientations and social identities may have played an important role in shaping how citizens responded to the pandemic, and indeed our data show that this was the case for attitudinal change in

Southeast Asia. National identity, in particular, was associated with increased support for social policy, as individuals who reported they feel very close to their nations were significantly more likely to report increased support for various social policy initiatives in all cases except for Indonesia. For example, a Thai respondent who reported feeling 'extremely close' to their nation had a predicted probability of increased support of 52 per cent, while this figure dropped to only 38 per cent for respondents who said they do not feel close to their nation. These findings remind us of the importance of 'rally round the flag' effects in shaping pandemic responses, and we can hypothesise that attachment to national identity serves a similar role to that of institutional trust.[4]

As for political–ideological leanings, estimation results were strong for our measure of economic redistribution. In all surveys, individuals who said they support spending more to help those who are least well off, even if it means increasing taxes, were significantly more likely to say that they had become more supportive of welfare state expansion as a result of the pandemic. As shown in Figure 3.4, based on the Singaporean case, the predicted probability of reporting increased support for social policies rises steadily with support for economic redistribution, from 23 per cent to 47 per cent. This strong association and its consistency across the countries we studied indicates a strong role of previous ideological orientation in shaping how individuals evaluate the pandemic and conceptualise possible policy measures to mitigate the adverse impact that similar events may have in the future. However, partisanship, as measured by support for the incumbent president or prime minister, was not significantly associated with attitudinal change. With the exception of the Malaysian survey, respondents who approved of the incumbent were not any more or less likely to support expanded social policies than those who did not approve. This result may be explained by the fact that political party systems in Southeast Asia, while often polarised around political figures or social issues such as

Figure 3.4: Support for economic redistribution and attitudinal change

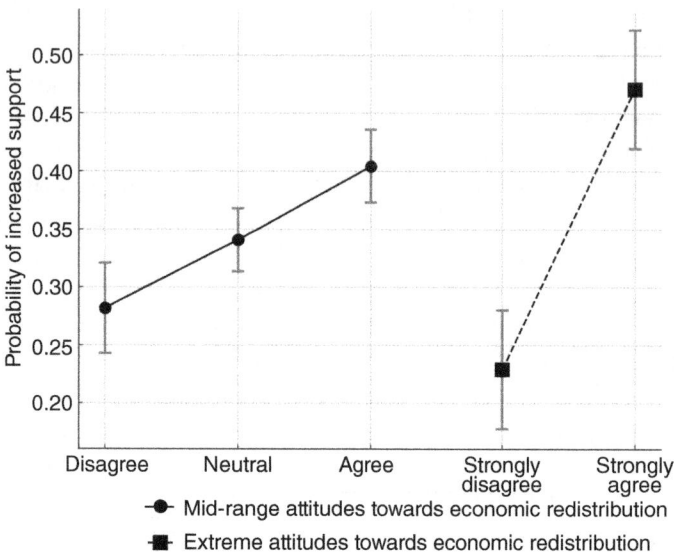

race and religion, rarely show programmatic differentiation among political parties on economic issues (Fossati, 2024b).

Finally, we can further analyse the impact of socioeconomic background factors, such as age, gender, education, and income, and assess if results from regression analysis aligns with the descriptive statistics discussed earlier. Indeed, results reported in Table 3.3 indicate the absence of strong patterns across countries, although there is some evidence that factors such as gender and education may matter in some contexts. Specifically, women respondents appear to be generally less likely to have reported becoming more supportive of expanded social policies, especially in the cases of Indonesia and Singapore, while college-educated respondents seem to have become more supportive of more generous welfare state arrangements compared with respondents with lower levels of education, a difference that was statistically significant in the surveys conducted in the Philippines and Thailand.

From attitudes to behaviours

The survey data we have collected allows us to study not only whether, and to what extent, the pandemic has changed attitudes, but also whether it has influenced behaviour. It should be noted that while attitudinal shifts and behavioural changes are often interrelated, they do not always move in tandem. For example, while individuals may express support for more comprehensive social policies, they might not necessarily vote for politicians who propose them or participate in advocacy campaigns. Second, studying behaviour through survey data presents distinct challenges, such as self-reporting biases, recall inaccuracies, and the difficulty of capturing nuanced behavioural changes through standardised questions. Nevertheless, even if behavioural change is not the primary focus of this book, studying changes in behaviour is important for a comprehensive understanding of the pandemic's impact, and an analysis of our survey data for this purpose could be a fruitful starting point to assess both the extent of behavioural change and its variation across individuals.

The specific behavioural changes we have chosen to investigate include preventive measures aimed at reducing infection rates, such as wearing masks in public, washing hands, and observing social distancing. We adopted this focus because understanding change in these behaviours has an obvious policy relevance, as they are direct responses to public health guidelines and can significantly influence the course of a pandemic. Furthermore, these behaviours may be considered as proxies for broader attitudinal shifts towards health consciousness and collective responsibility. To a certain degree, then, even if we are looking at very specific individual health-related behaviours, their evolution may signal broader cultural and social shifts. At the same time, however, we should acknowledge that changes in preventive behaviours may not necessarily correlate with the changes in opinions about social policy analysed in the previous chapter. No theoretical expectation suggests that, for example, individuals who have significantly changed their health-related behaviour would be more likely to support expanding existing social policies. We therefore analyse the two spheres of individual-level change – attitudinal and behavioural – separately, recognising that they constitute distinct and equally important dimensions of how people have responded to the pandemic.

We asked four questions about changes in preventive behaviour. Specifically, we asked if, after the end of the acute phase of the COVID-19 pandemic, respondents were more likely to observe social distancing, wash their hands frequently, wear a mask in public, and avoid large gatherings of people than they had been before the pandemic. For each of these variables, we built a binary indicator that tracks if individuals responded affirmatively, and the results are displayed in Figure 3.5, disaggregated by country. Overall, across the five samples, respondents were substantially more likely to report washing their hands more frequently than before the pandemic (66 per cent affirmative answers) than engaging more often in

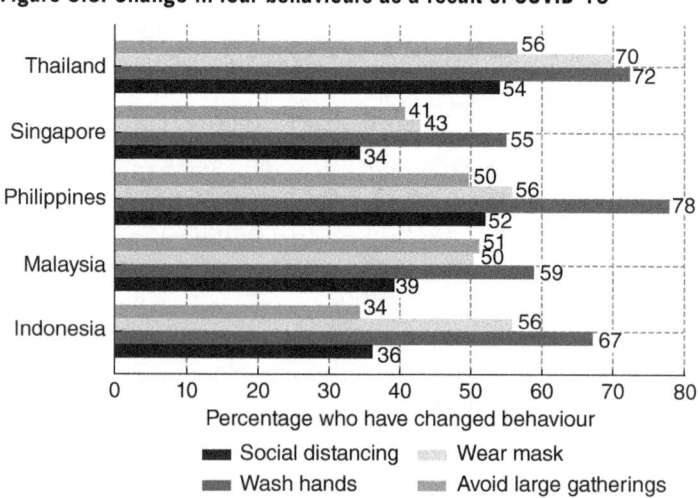

Figure 3.5: Change in four behaviours as a result of COVID-19

wearing a mask (55 per cent), avoiding large crowds (47 per cent), and observing social distancing (43 per cent). These findings suggest that while a substantial portion of populations in Southeast Asia increased some preventive health practices, there was variation across these specific behaviours. Change in the simple behaviour of hand washing, long associated with personal hygiene, appears to be the most common and possibly the most enduring, while other more cumbersome measures associated with the emergency phase of the pandemic seem less likely to become ingrained as preventive measures. In general, then, we find evidence that Southeast Asians have changed some of their behaviours, but that the change has been selective and varies across individuals.

To synthesise the data related to health behaviour into a single variable of behavioural change, we built an additive index based on the four questions. The index measures how many questions were answered affirmatively. Across the five samples, about 18 per cent of respondents reported no change at all in behaviour, while 20 per cent reported changing one behaviour, 20 per cent reported changing two behaviours, 18 per cent reported changing three behaviours, and 24 per cent reported carrying out all four preventive health measures more often than they did before the pandemic. This indicator thus shows that behavioural responses to the pandemic varied substantially across individuals, as only some of those we sampled reported a sustained change in their health practices, while others, after the end of the acute phase of the pandemic, reverted to their previous routines rather than sustaining any significant changes. As Figure 3.5 suggests, this indicator also varied significantly across countries. Thailand and the Philippines are the countries in which preventive health behaviour appears to have changed most substantially, with 33 per cent and 30 per cent of respondents reporting four changes, respectively, while the figure dropped to 22 per cent in Malaysia, 19 per cent in Indonesia, and only 17 per cent in Singapore. Identifying one specific factor explaining variation across the cases is of course challenging, since such differences may reflect variation in public health strategies, cultural attitudes towards health practices, prior levels of preventive behaviours, and the severity of the pandemic's impact in each nation. Yet these patterns do remind us of the importance of context-specific elements in accounting for behavioural responses to the pandemic, and, by extension, their importance in promoting and maintaining public health behaviours in the aftermath of a global health crisis.

We used this aggregate index for regression analysis, as we estimated a series of ordered logistic models in which behavioural change is a function of the same covariates used in statistical analysis in the previous section. Results are reported in Table 3.4. They show interesting commonalities and differences when compared with the analysis of attitudinal change. In general, we can see how several covariates that were crucial for explaining attitudinal change do not seem so significant as drivers of behavioural change. Perhaps most notably, support for economic redistribution, which was positive and significant in all models estimated in the previous section, had no effect on behaviour in four of the five countries, and a similar pattern was found for attachment to national identity and evaluations of performance in managing the pandemic, both factors that were found to be drivers of attitudinal change. Similarly, support for the incumbent president or prime minister and trust in public institutions were only significantly associated with higher adoption of preventive behaviour in two countries. We therefore find that, in sharp contrast with the results from the analysis performed in the previous section, ideological and political orientations do not appear to be highly significant determinants of behavioural change.

While cognitive ideological–partisan orientations and assessments of institutional performance were mostly unrelated to behavioural change, a strong effect was observed for the covariates measuring the more affective dimension of pandemic-related attitudes. Exposure to the pandemic

Table 3.4: Determinants of behavioural change in five countries

Variables	(1) Indonesia	(2) Malaysia	(3) Philippines	(4) Singapore	(5) Thailand
Exposure to COVID-19	0.116*** (0.0472)	0.0625 (0.0530)	0.0155 (0.0494)	0.230*** (0.0597)	0.116*** (0.0489)
Trust in public institutions	0.0491 (0.0390)	0.0767*** (0.0373)	0.0578 (0.0340)	0.0414 (0.0408)	0.0852*** (0.0341)
Evaluation of COVID-19 performance	0.117 (0.0662)	−0.195*** (0.0748)	−0.0205 (0.0560)	−0.0688 (0.0768)	−0.0254 (0.0648)
Support for the president = 1	0.338*** (0.120)	0.132 (0.110)	0.198 (0.110)	0.366*** (0.126)	0.172 (0.140)
Worried about disease risk	0.135*** (0.0357)	0.117*** (0.0375)	0.114*** (0.0356)	0.157*** (0.0365)	0.128*** (0.0326)
Ideology (support for redistribution)	0.0484 (0.0435)	−0.119*** (0.0461)	0.0530 (0.0416)	0.0780 (0.0477)	0.0755 (0.0401)
National attachment	0.00182 (0.0758)	0.198*** (0.0859)	−0.120 (0.0773)	−0.124 (0.0908)	0.0425 (0.0772)
Age	−0.00272 (0.00432)	−0.00974*** (0.00375)	0.00531 (0.00408)	0.00363 (0.00386)	0.0109*** (0.00444)

(continued)

Table 3.4: Determinants of behavioural change in five countries (continued)

Variables	(1) Indonesia	(2) Malaysia	(3) Philippines	(4) Singapore	(5) Thailand
Gender = 2, Female	0.740*** (0.109)	0.137 (0.107)	0.243*** (0.106)	0.401*** (0.109)	0.0772 (0.106)
College education = 1	0.0354 (0.113)	−0.0684 (0.106)	−0.0601 (0.116)	0.298*** (0.111)	0.171 (0.117)
Income	−0.0281 (0.0514)	−0.206*** (0.0567)	0.0554 (0.0615)	−0.0960 (0.0603)	−0.0573 (0.0570)
/cut1	0.649 (0.349)	−1.796*** (0.371)	−0.609 (0.341)	0.592 (0.428)	−0.292 (0.310)
/cut2	1.874*** (0.351)	−0.963*** (0.367)	0.672*** (0.337)	1.582*** (0.430)	0.810*** (0.306)
/cut3	2.872*** (0.356)	−0.0947 (0.365)	1.525*** (0.339)	2.305*** (0.432)	1.681*** (0.309)
/cut4	3.817*** (0.364)	0.763*** (0.367)	2.335*** (0.343)	3.231*** (0.437)	2.604*** (0.314)
Observations	1,200	1,200	1,200	1,200	1,200
Log-likelihood	−1,860	−1,886	−1,862	−1,865	−1,812

Notes: Standard errors are given in parentheses. *** $p < 0.05$.

has a positive effect on increased adoption of preventative measures in three surveys – namely, Indonesia, Singapore, and Thailand. For example, the predicted probability of a respondent based in Thailand reporting they changed all four preventive behaviours was about 31 per cent for individuals who had not experienced any major disruption because of the pandemic, but rose to 41 per cent in respondents who had lost loved ones, their job, and access to healthcare during the pandemic. This illustration shows how powerful the effect of individual experiences with the pandemic can be in fostering behavioural change, and results for our indicator of worrying about infections further documents the importance of affective factors. In all surveys, individuals who were more worried about the risk of contracting various infectious diseases were more likely to report having increased the practice of preventive health measures. This relationship is displayed in Figure 3.6 (based on the Indonesian data), showing that predicted probabilities of changing all four

Figure 3.6: Anxiety about infection and behavioural change

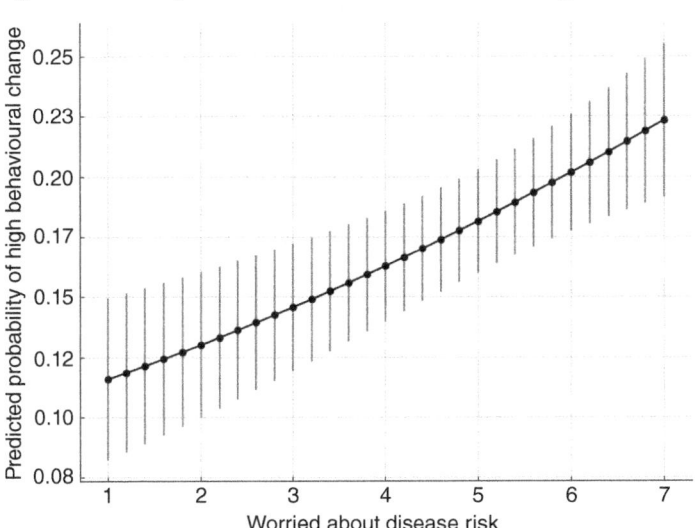

behaviours rose steadily as a function of increased worry about infection risk.

Finally, while most sociodemographic variables were not consistently associated with change in behaviour across the five samples, we found that the estimated coefficient for gender was positive and significant in three surveys. Female respondents in Indonesia, the Philippines, and Singapore were significantly more likely than men to report that they had changed their health preventive behaviours because of the pandemic, while results were not statistically significant in Malaysia and Thailand. The positive finding is consistent with other studies that have similarly found, using cross-national data, that there was a difference in health behaviour between genders during the acute phase of the pandemic (Galasso et al, 2020). They suggest that, to an extent, such differences may have extended beyond the pandemic emergency to become entrenched. Identifying the exact factors explaining gender differences in COVID-19 preventive behaviour is beyond the scope of our work, but existing research has suggested women's higher risk perception, caregiving roles, greater health awareness, and economic vulnerability as well as the expectation that women will prioritise family health and well-being may all play a role.

Conclusion

In this chapter, we leveraged our original survey dataset with three goals in mind. First, we assessed the extent to which ordinary citizens in Southeast Asia shifted their views on key social policy issues as a result of the COVID-19 pandemic. Second, we analysed the individual-level factors driving this attitudinal change, investigating variations within the five societies we studied. Finally, we extended this analysis to examine changes in health-related behaviour, identifying both patterns and predictors of behavioural adaptation across the different national contexts.

To summarise our key findings, we have documented that citizens across Southeast Asia have generally become more supportive of inclusive and comprehensive social policies due to the pandemic's impact. Surveying respondents on various aspects of social policy, we found that majorities in each country have shown increased support for welfare policies, particularly in areas such as government involvement in healthcare, enhanced health and social insurance, and access to essential services like childcare. But we have also identified significant cross-country variation, with attitudinal shifts being more pronounced in some cases, such as Indonesia, and more modest in others, such as Singapore. This variation underscores the influence of local contexts in shaping public responses to social welfare issues, a crucial issue to which the next chapter is dedicated.

We have then performed a full analysis of the drivers through which the COVID-19 pandemic has facilitated attitudinal and behavioural change. We found that personal exposure to the pandemic and anxiety about infection risks are significant determinants of changes in both attitudes towards social policy and health preventive behaviour. This strongly suggests that direct experience and perceived vulnerability play critical roles in shaping individuals' responses to the crisis at various levels. Yet we have also found important differences between the determinants of attitudinal and behavioural change. While health preventive behaviours are largely predicted by personal exposure and risk perception alone, changes in social policy attitudes represent a more complex phenomenon, significantly influenced by ideological factors, assessments of institutional performance, trust in institutions, and even feelings of national attachment. This divergence indicates that while behaviour may be more directly tied to immediate concerns about health and safety, attitudes towards broader social policies are shaped by deeper, more entrenched, and more stable beliefs as well as trust in societal and political structures.

FOUR

Institutions, politics, and social welfare

In this chapter, we explore the institutions (and institutional obstacles) which, in the five Southeast Asian countries we studied, led to a largely 'negative' policy outcome of the pandemic in terms of greater institutionalisation of and/or sustained increase in social welfare provision. Despite the generally strong citizen support for greater state welfarism, as shown in the discussion of the results of our original survey in Chapter 3, we focus here on the institutional factors which inhibited the short-term expansion in welfare measures during the pandemic from translating into longer-term policy change leading to greater social inclusion. It is argued that the key common factor is these states' ability to deflect (albeit in a variety of ways) citizen demands in order to quickly return to lower, pre-COVID-19 levels of welfare provision. What the lack of policy change in all of these countries demonstrates is that through various stratagems – ideological hegemony, clientelistic networks, and regime survival strategies – they were able to re-equilibrate their political systems and retrench social assistance largely to pre-pandemic levels.

We demonstrate in this chapter how new policy outcomes emerging from critical junctures are not inevitable but, rather, an outcome of permissive conditions providing the opportunity for change and the productive conditions enabling that change to occur, as discussed in Chapter 2. It is shown how changing popular attitudes, as documented in the previous chapter, and civil society mobilisation, discussed in this chapter, which might be interpreted as favouring institutional change, ultimately lost out to conservative, pro-establishment forces wishing a return to the status quo ante in terms of social welfare provision. The crisis phase of the pandemic in which social welfare measures were quite rapidly and extensively expanded in all these Southeast countries during a period of uncertainty and institutional fluidity resulted not in lasting policy transformation but re-equilibration. Such 'negative cases' of policy change during a critical juncture increases analytical leverage because it reveals what otherwise would likely remain hidden if the concentration was only on cases leading to major transformation (Capoccia, 2015).

As we show here, in Singapore, despite the rollout of much-expanded social relief measures by the ruling People's Action Party (PAP), the end of the pandemic led to renewed warnings about a 'welfare trap' which would supposedly snare the country in a cycle of lower growth, once again demonstrating the power of a neoliberal technocratic ideology in the city-state. In Indonesia and the Philippines, populist presidents went from denialism about the pandemic to major increases in spending to combat it. But this largely represented a temporary increase in patronage distribution used to build and consolidate political support, not to increases in programmatic welfare spending. In Thailand and Malaysia, conservative elites facing severe legitimacy crises coalesced with formerly reformist partners who offered temporary cash handouts or made appeals to particular ethno-religious constituencies in an attempt to quickly gain political support rather than addressing long-term structural problems though reforms, including expansion of universal welfare. As a result, what could have been a window of opportunity for a sustained expansion of social welfare systems in Southeast Asia soon closed, leading to a return to pre-pandemic levels of social provision.

The marginalisation of agents of change in Southeast Asia

There was an often abrupt decline of socialism and communism in Southeast Asia during the Cold War, often through brutal crackdowns (Hewison and Rodan, 2011). In some cases, this repression continues to the present, particularly in the Philippines with an anti-terrorism law targeting legal Left-wing activists supporting the communist movement through non-violent means (International Crisis Group, 2024). Across the region, this repression badly weakened the traditional socialist Left, which has historically been the strongest advocate for more comprehensive social welfare policy. In terms of critical junctures, discussed in Chapter 2, this can be understood as a disadvantageous antecedent condition for more institutionalised and expanded social policies following increased social expenditures during the pandemic.

This void in Left socialist politics has often been filled by the rise of an extensive and often highly mobilised civil society, albeit to a more limited extent in Singapore (Tan, 2010). Following Rodan (2022), the aim of civil society activists, if not always the outcome of their efforts, is to influence the state's exercise of power, including often pushing for greater social inclusion. Civil society in the region consists of anti-liberal groups competing with more liberal ones, with some groups broadly secular in orientation and others highly religious (Rodan, 2022). Civil society encompasses a broad political space, including but not limited to civil society organisations focused on labour (including unions), religion, other identity issues, and in particular policy advocacy.

The rise of a liberal–progressive civil society paralleled re-democratisation across the region, beginning with 'people power' in the Philippines in 1986, the Black May uprising in Thailand in 1992, Reformasi in Indonesia in 1998, and the decades-long democratisation movement in Malaysia which resulted in a (partial) democratic transition in 2018. Yet, the landslide of democratic backsliding has often eroded the influence of civil society in the region. In Thailand, the 2014 coup largely demobilised civil society, but the manipulated 2019 elections helped spur massive youth protests from 2020 to 2022, breaking the taboo in Thai politics of criticising the oversized role of monarchy and the military (Thompson and Cheng, 2022). In the Philippines in 2016, newly elected president Rodrigo R. Duterte launched a brutal but popular 'war on drugs' while targeting independent media and activist groups, leaving civil society 'bowed, bent, and broken' (Iglesias, 2022; Arugay and Baquisal, 2023: 328). In 2017, Indonesian president Joko Widodo (popularly known as Jokowi) began a crackdown on Islamists in the name of defending pluralism, but this severely eroded civil liberties in the country and also targeted non-Islamist groups, undermining the strength of civil society and leading the country to become virtually opposition-less by the end of Jokowi's term (Berenschot, 2023; Fossati, 2024a). In Malaysia in 2020, a reformist government was toppled (Weiss, 2022). But civil society protests were revived during the pandemic and contributed to snap general elections being called, which resulted in a coalition government between long-time oppositionists and the former ruling party (Panneerselvam and Tayeb, 2023). In Singapore, after the 2011 elections in which opposition parties had performed somewhat better in a heavily gerrymandered electoral system, there was a steady erosion of already severely limited civil liberties in the city-state (Tan and Preece, 2024).

This weakening of civil society as a potential 'change agent' in most of the Southeast Asian countries considered in this study largely marginalised it as a possible 'permissive' condition for increasingly institutionalised and expanded social policies after COVID-19. Major groups in civil society across these Southeast Asian countries, both secular and religious, often represented the collective actor most strongly advocating greater social welfare and inclusion (Rodan, 2022). The disempowerment of civil society does not necessarily determine the absence of substantive and sustained improvements in social welfare. Reforms such as the gradual expansion towards universal healthcare in Indonesia (Fossati, 2017) and the introduction of Thailand's 30-baht universal coverage scheme (Selway, 2011) illustrate that meaningful increases in healthcare coverage can occur even in the absence of strong civil society pressure. However, the limited role of civil society did constrain the transmission of the shifting public attitudes documented in the previous chapter into government deliberations and potential policy change. In the absence of assertive societal actors, the link between changing public preferences and institutional responses remained weak.

Singapore: Bolstering technocracy and rejecting 'welfarism'

There is little dispute in the literature that, overall, the PAP-led Singapore government performed relatively well during the pandemic, measured both in general terms, by its maintaining economic growth and achieving a lower-than-usual death rate, as well as by several more specific measures, such as testing, contact tracing, and vaccination rates (Woo, 2020). However, a potentially deadly chink in the city-state's anti-COVID-19 armour was the high number of infections among economically underprivileged migrant workers living in crowded dormitories early on in the pandemic, which underlined the state's neglect of and societal discrimination against this group (Han, 2020). Nonetheless, strong state capacity meant that through contact tracing, effective medical care, and, later, high vaccination rates, fatality rates remained low in a healthcare system that held up well under the strains of the pandemic (Woo, 2020). Even the death rate among migrant workers was not higher than it was in the rest of the Singapore population, which however 'may be partly attributed to the fact that migrant workers and younger imported cases were largely protected by their young age and few medical comorbidities' (Ngiam et al, 2021: 335).

The key to Singapore's relative pandemic success was not only in reacting quickly to the pandemic, securing its borders, and ordering a sweeping lockdown; it was also that – unlike in other countries in Southeast Asia and most other countries globally – once testing and contact tracing capacity improved, lockdowns were eased so as to not severely affect economic growth and that there was healthcare capacity to deal with severe cases and later ensure a rapid and widespread vaccine rollout. Singapore thus avoided the overly strict, one-size-fits-all lockdowns and/or social distancing approaches that in much of Asia, Europe, and North America resulted in severe economic slowdown.

The pandemic enabled the PAP-government to bolster popular perceptions of its rule as technocratic, thus preserving high levels of public trust in its governance despite 'stark socio-economic disparity exacerbated by the crisis' (De Visser and Straughan, 2021: 222). This finding is also borne out in our survey findings on high levels of public trust in Singapore, as shown in Chapter 3. This positive perception of the PAP's competency and efficiency meant that it suffered only minor losses and retained nearly 90 per cent of parliamentary seats in the 2020 election despite this being called in the midst of the worst phase of the pandemic (Oliver and Ostwald, 2022). The PAP's electoral domination, based in part on extensive gerrymandering, was similar to all other of the city-state's general elections since independence, although with a slightly smaller supermajority than in the 2015 election held amid public nostalgia for the country's 'founding father' and long-time PAP Prime Minister Lee Kuan Yew, who passed shortly before the polls were held.

The Singapore government spent an additional SGD 72.3 billion (USD 54.6 billion), nearly 20 per cent of annual gross domestic product (GDP), in 2020 to 2021 to deal with the pandemic and to provide increased social welfare provision for those most adversely affected by it. The fiscal stimulus helped limit the economic decline in the pandemic's first year. It is estimated that from February 2020 to March 2022, the government spent over SGD 28 billion (about USD 20 billion) on the Jobs Support Scheme, which helped save an estimated 165,000 jobs in 2020 (Inland Revenue Authority, 2022). Government programmes targeted the most vulnerable sectors, in particular small firms and lower-income households (Ministry of Finance, 2021). Other schemes included the Wage Credit Scheme to increase workers' wages, the SkillsFuture Credit top-up scheme for courses designed to 'upskill' workers, the Senior Worker Support Package for workers over 55, the Part-Time Re-Employment Grant, designed to entice companies to formalise part-time re-employment, the Workfare Income Supplement for Singaporeans earning in the bottom 20 per cent, and various general voucher schemes for the general adult Singaporean population (Ministry of Finance [Singapore], 2020). Additional measures followed, including the Self-Employed Person Income Relief Scheme, support for Muslim religious teachers, the Point-to-Point Support Package for eligible taxi and private hire drivers, additional subsidies to the arts and culture sector aimed particularly at upskilling and digitisation efforts, rental waivers for eligible tenants in government properties and for stallholders in hawker (local merchant) centres, and property tax rebates for commercial and non-commercial buildings (Ministry of Finance [Singapore], 2020).

Singapore's highly responsive set of measures can be seen across five budgets, with over SGD 100 billion (USD 74 billion) allocated for economic stimulus and social support packages as well as the rapid expansion of public health sector capacities (Ministry of Finance [Singapore], 2021: 2). But as the pandemic receded, Singapore wound down most of its welfare and stimulus packages, although the commitments arising from infrastructure-building initiatives had a longer-term fiscal impact.

This indicates that the need for massive social assistance during COVID-19 did not lead to the PAP abandoning its ideological hostility to 'welfarism' and the need to maintain the image of Singapore as a 'meritocratic' society in which inequality is a natural outcome of individual differences in talent, skill, and application. A constant throughout this period of increased social welfare spending was the PAP government's stress on the need for Singaporeans to retrain and 'upskill' to ensure that they would remain attractive employees for businesses – domestic and global (Ministry of Finance [Singapore], 2020). This was evidence of the government using the pandemic to reinforce its 'ideology of pragmatism', which had made 'more palatable ... its association with neo-liberal globalisation, which in turn obscures the crisis tendencies and exploitative goals of global capitalism and the real political goals of the PAP government' (Tan, 2012: 71). It is further demonstration of what Tan (2012: 87, 89) has described as the PAP-government's 'continuous ideological work to contain and dissipate opposition' by prizing its 'authoritarian, meritocratic and technocratic' governance. As shown in Chapter 3, the attitudes of most Singaporeans appear to be in alignment with this neoliberal technocratic ideology of small government given that, among the five countries analysed in the book, respondents from the city-state had the lowest share supporting substantial expansion of social welfare in the wake of the pandemic.

Given this strong ideological foundation and the lack of effective opposing social and political constituencies, the Singapore government had no difficulty in quickly discontinuing socially inclusive policy measures in the name of restoring fiscal stability and reinforcing its ideological opposition to 'welfarism'. A notable, temporary exception was – in an apparent nod to rising inequality in the city-state, which had been aggravated by the pandemic – the continuation of the Community Development Council voucher scheme designed to help lower-income households defray the cost of living and buttress hawkers until the end of 2025 (Community Development Council, 2024).

The government has continued to make familiar pronouncements about needing to avoid a 'welfarism trap', which, it was feared, would weaken the incentive to work and hobble entrepreneurship – former Prime Minister Lee Kuan Yew had repeatedly warned about this issue (Tze, 2016). In the run up to the 2025 General Election, Prime Minister Lawrence Wong defended an increase in the regressive Goods and Services Tax (GST) and criticised an opposition proposal for a universal minimum wage saying there is no 'free lunch' in Singapore (Straits Times, 2025). The institutional and ideological dominance of the PAP and extensive state capacity have served to pre-empt any demands for the sustained expansion of the country's social welfare system.

Indonesia and the Philippines: Pandemic populism and increased patronage

Both the Philippine's Rodrigo Duterte (president from 2016 to 2022) and Indonesia's Joko Widodo (president from 2014 to 2024) have been characterised by scholars as populist leaders, albeit with Duterte being called a 'penal' or 'violent' populist for his bloody 'war on drugs' (Curato, 2016; Thompson, 2021) and Jokowi a 'polite' or 'developmentalist' populist for his more economically oriented approach (Warburton, 2016). Both were local political outsiders who denounced corrupt and incompetent national elites before rising to presidential power based on their track record as mayor (Garcia, 2024). Both also enjoyed record popularity as presidents despite considerable democratic backsliding during their respective presidencies (Fossati et al, 2022; Thompson, 2023).

Similar to US President Donald Trump and Brazilian President Jair Bolsonaro, Duterte and Widodo were initially 'denialists' or 'medical populists' at the outset of the pandemic (Lasco, 2020; Mietzner, 2020). They ignored science, denied the severity of the crisis, and dramatised their unscientific pandemic responses based on conspiratorial 'knowledge claims', which allowed them to shift the blame to others in order to deflect from their ineffective COVID-19 response. In the case of Indonesia, Widodo's democratic backsliding 'produced intensifying populist anti-scientism, religious conservatism, religio-political polarization, corruption and clientelism', with these factors combining 'into a toxic mix that severely constrained Indonesia's ability to effectively respond to a massive external shock such as COVID-19' (Mietzner, 2020: 227). In the Philippines, Duterte initially joked about the pandemic and claimed Filipinos' strong antibodies would make them highly resistant to the new virus (Hapal, 2021). Duterte 'stigmatised public concern and caution by characterising it as a hysterical overreaction' and 'feminising' those warning of the dangers to public health (Parmanand, 2020).

In contrast to the Singaporean leadership, Widodo and Duterte lost valuable time when they were 'in denial' about the pandemic's severity and the need to act fast and decisively to slow its spread. Even after they eventually recognised the dangers of COVID-19, they still failed to act in a technocratically rational fashion. Instead, both leaders adopted a militarised approach that proved largely counterproductive.

Duterte securitised the complex pandemic crisis, opting for highly militarised and indiscriminate enforcement, bullying government officials to comply while scapegoating an 'unseen enemy', dangerously reckless individuals (known in Filipino as *pasaway*) who supposedly defied government lockdown orders in order to deflect public attention from policy failures which can be understood as 'brute force governance' (Hapal, 2021: 224; Thompson, 2022: 399). He 'shapeshifted' from 'the invincible man' who did not fear COVID-19 to his nation's 'tough protector' in the fight against it (Parmanand, 2020). When Duterte finally did act in mid-March 2020, he imposed one of the world's longest, most inflexible, and most severe lockdowns that, nonetheless, failed to keep down excess deaths because of a lack of testing, disregard for expert medical advice, over-reliance on the military, and a slow vaccine rollout (Mendoza, 2021). He declared a national state of calamity and had a pliant Congress give him emergency powers to combat the virus. The lockdown was carried out in a highly militarised fashion with heavy reliance on the police and armed forces, as testing for and tracing of COVID-19 cases lagged badly.

Although he was no longer a pandemic denialist, Duterte's response still involved blame shifting and used impractical one-size-fits-all lockdowns. Already cowed during Duterte's first years in office, civil society was further weakened by the highly securitised pandemic lockdown, which labelled any dissent as a threat to national security (Hapal, 2021). Using methods developed during his bloody 'war on drugs', Duterte scapegoated *pasaways* for the spread of the pandemic despite data showing Filipinos were among the world's most obedient citizens in following lockdown instructions (Hapal, 2021). He blamed governance failures during the pandemic on local governments, although they were given confusing national instructions and the distribution of subsidies from the national level was slow and lists of intended beneficiaries were incomplete (Hutchcroft and Gera, 2022). Long and inflexible lockdowns led to soaring poverty and record hunger levels with huge job losses and lost economic opportunities (Teehankee, 2020). Yet, at over 80 per cent, Duterte's approval ratings remained robust (Thompson, 2022).

In Indonesia, Jokowi also changed course, although in this case it was only several months after the outbreak of the pandemic. Moving away from denialism but, like Duterte, insisting on a militarised response, Jokowi gave the army and intelligence services an enlarged role. Yet, unlike Duterte, he moved to quickly open up the country economically, avoiding the long, restrictive lockdown Duterte had imposed on the Philippines. Fearing damage to the economy, Jokowi opted for localised, partial, and short-term lockdowns rather than a national shutdown, but this proved to be of very limited utility (Setijadi, 2021). The consequence of this rash opening was unsurprisingly a high excess death rate. He discarded 'many aspects of his broader social and political reform agenda and focused single-mindedly on what is most important to him: the economy and development' (Fealy, 2020: 302). Most public health experts remained critical of Jokowi's pandemic policies, however. Mitigation measures were inadequate and inconsistent with too much emphasis placed on an early vaccine rollout to limit the spread of the pandemic when the country had already been reopened. Jokowi's developmentalist populism, with its 'core preoccupations with material prosperity and advancement', became even clearer during the pandemic due to his 'constant exhortations for Indonesians to be disciplined, to take on new, more productive mindsets and habits, and to not be downcast by the current crisis but to rise above it and behold the nation's glimmering prospects' (Fealy, 2020: 302). This was evident in his prioritisation of 'economic recovery over public health', his mobilisation of the military to enforce COVID-19 protocols, and his willingness to intimidate government critics (in particular, by using extralegal means to suppress a supposed Islamist threat during the health emergency; Fealy, 2020: 302).

Despite its 'devastating' consequences to Indonesia, Jokowi was able to use the pandemic as an 'opportunity to further consolidate power', justified by the need to maintain order, protect health, and boost economic recovery (Setijadi, 2021: 299). Civil society, which had been on the defensive since President Jokowi began cracking down on Islamists in 2017 but soon widened its approach to make a more general attack on opposition, was further marginalised by his administration during the pandemic (Fealy, 2020). By the time the pandemic wound down, the country had become an 'opposition-less democracy' (Berenschot, 2023). Hence, similar to the Philippines' counter-institutional approach, civil society forces that might have pushed for enhanced social welfare were largely neutralised, as Jokowi had largely negated opposition power.

Globally, opinion polls showed the pandemic 'reversed the rise of populism', including diminishing people's 'approval of populist leaders' (Foa et al, 2022). But for both Duterte and Jokowi, it actually served to *buttress* their popularity. As Arguelles (2021: 257) notes, in the case of Duterte, 'rather than being a curse ... the pandemic turned out to be a gift'. For Jokowi, the tendencies he displayed during the pandemic 'have been apparent for several years, but they are now far more pronounced as he strives ... to secure his place in history as a great president' (Fealy, 2020: 302). The Indonesian and Philippine presidents effectively used the pandemic as an opportunity to renew their populist mandates for their illiberal agendas.

Both Duterte and Jokowi launched major social welfare initiatives during COVID-19. In the Philippines, two fiscal stimulus packages (Bayanihan Acts I and II) were passed in 2020, with the second one extended through 2021. Together, they cost PHP 602.1 billion (USD 12.1 billion), equivalent to 3.1 per cent of the country's 2021 GDP (Basilio et al, 2022: 6). They provided direct cash assistance to low-income workers – such as domestic helpers, subcontractual workers, homeworkers, drivers and public utility operators, microentrepreneurs, farmers, daily wage earners, and stranded workers – as well as other vulnerable sections of the population (including indigent senior citizens, persons with disabilities, pregnant women, solo parents, overseas workers in distress, indigenous peoples, and the homeless; Asian Development Bank, 2020). Hard-hit sectors of the economy – such as agriculture, transportation, and tourism – were also targeted. Yet implementation was flawed because of reliance on the Listahanan – outdated lists from the National Household Targeting System for Poverty Reduction which only partially covered those who were most adversely affected by the pandemic (Eadie and Yacub, 2024). Given the problematic nature of this national data, implementation of much of the pandemic social assistance was handed over to the discretion of local government units, where the failure to reach many needy recipients quickly became evident (World Bank, 2020). Duterte's bullying of local politicians enabled him to shift the blame for implementation failures of social protection policies onto them rather than admitting that these problems had originated at the national level (Hutchcroft and Gera, 2022).

In Indonesia, the Jokowi administration expanded existing social protection programmes, including conditional cash transfers for poor families, food vouchers and rice assistance, and business loans (Androff and Abbas, 2023). His administration also created a major unemployment programme (the Jaminan Kehilangan Pekerjaan), a rare example in the region of a new policy enacted during the pandemic (Yuda, 2022: 309). These were part of an array of government responses that, besides social assistance, included stimulus packages which aimed to stabilise the country economically and cast a wide safety net for vulnerable populations – a deep recession was avoided and the overall government spending increased by 61.5 per cent in 2020 over 2019 (Indrawati, 2024). The National Economic Recovery (PEN) programme provided IDR 576 trillion (about USD 41 billion) of fiscal support in 2020, aiming to cover extra expenditures on healthcare and social assistance and to help businesses affected by the pandemic. Funding for the PEN programme was increased in 2021 by nearly 30 per cent, to IDR 775 trillion, in the hope of jump-starting economic recovery and supporting job creation. Despite these measures, two million Indonesians lost their jobs, resulting in a 1 per cent increase in the unemployment rate and 2.5 million people falling into poverty (Ministry of Finance [Indonesia], 2021; Sit, 2022).

However, Indonesia and the Philippines significantly reduced social and other governmental expenditure once the pandemic eased. In the Philippines, the central government deficit declined from 5.4 per cent of GDP in 2022 to 4.6 per cent in 2023, with it estimated to fall further to 3.6 per cent by 2026 (FitchRatings, 2025). In Indonesia, the government budget deficit declined from 2.4 per cent of GDP in 2022 to 1.7 per cent in 2023, although it was projected to have increased somewhat to 2.3 per cent of GDP in 2024 and to 2.8 per cent of GDP in 2025 (Indrawati, 2024; OECD, 2025). While social protection expenditure appears to have remained high in Indonesia after the height of the pandemic, this was misleading, as more than half of the money spent had been earmarked for subsidies, particularly energy subsidies, including for liquid petroleum gas, electricity, and fuel (Indrawati, 2024: 17). If subsidies are excluded, Indonesia's expenditures for social protection were only 1 per cent of GDP in 2022, lagging behind Singapore (6.2 per cent), Malaysia (5.5 per cent), and the Philippines (3.8 per cent; OECD, 2022). This low level of social protection expenditure in Indonesia came despite unemployment surpassing 7 per cent and the poverty rate climbing to over 10 per cent during the pandemic (Sit, 2022). In the Philippines, an estimated 2.3 million people fell into poverty during the pandemic, meaning the total rose to almost 20 million or 18.1 per cent of the population, up from 16.7 per cent in 2018 (Reuters, 2022). These figures highlight the power of institutions and elites to sideline increased social welfare, despite heightened poverty levels, once the worst of the pandemic had passed.

Social assistance during the pandemic in the Philippines had already assumed a strongly clientelist character given the decentralised nature of distribution of assistance, inadequate lists of potential beneficiaries provided by the national government, and political interference at both the national and local levels (Hutchcroft and Gera, 2022; Eadie and Yacub, 2024). One of the biggest corruption scandals of the Duterte administration involved the procurement of overpriced medical equipment of inferior quality during the pandemic, which became known as the Pharmally scandal, named after the pharmaceutical company in question (Cepeda, 2021). A senate 'blue ribbon' committee investigation probed the role in the scandal of close Duterte adviser Michael Yang, among others. Duterte barred cabinet officials from participating in the hearings and attacked the senators involved, and the panel chair subsequently lost his re-election bid in the face of criticism from Duterte (Gonzales, 2021). In 2023, the chief anti-corruption agency, the Office of the Ombudsman, found several government executives guilty of administrative offences and recommended the filing of criminal graft charges against them and several Pharmally executives.

The patronage character of COVID-19 assistance lived on after the pandemic and was perhaps the most important legacy of the pandemic in the Philippines. For the 2024 budget, modelled on COVID-19 assistance, the Marcos administration allocated about 9 per cent of the national government budget for 'assistance to the poor and households with insufficient income' through the Income Aid to the Poor (Ayuda sa Kapos ang Kita) programme, with target beneficiaries receiving a one-time cash assistance of PHP 5,000 (Cervantes, 2023). A critical senator (Imee Marcos, the president's disaffected sister) challenged the programme for being 'undefined, unnamed, unfamiliar with no guidelines whatsoever with no target beneficiaries, and … just left open' and at the discretion of the House Speaker, Martin Romualdez, first cousin of the Marcoses (Bordey, 2024). Such a major budget allocation came as expenditures on the country's supposedly universal healthcare scheme were 'put under the knife', slashed by nearly 5 per cent in the 2024 budget (Piedad, 2023). There was an outcry about the 2025 budget when a 'zero subsidy' was provided for the country's national insurance scheme, PhilHealth, with one critic saying the cut left 'senior citizens, PWDs [persons with disabilities], and indigent Filipinos vulnerable and exposed' (Flores, 2024).

In a parallel fashion, the Corruption Eradication Commission (KPK) in Indonesia investigated misappropriations of government-funded social aid, known as *bansos*, during the COVID-19 pandemic. While officially under the Social Affairs Ministry, this form of social assistance was initiated during the pandemic by President Jokowi, leading him to be widely known as the '*bansos* president'. In mid-2024, one official was imprisoned for eight years by the Jakarta Corruption Court, while five others were sentenced to between five and six years after being found guilty of corruption in regards to diverting money which was supposed to be distributed as *bansos*. In an earlier corruption case, in 2021, Juliari Batubara, the social affairs minister, was convicted of accepting IDR 32.48 billion in bribes from private vendors supplying COVID-19 food aid and was sentenced to a 12-year prison term. Malfeasance in social aid distribution was also at the centre of two cases filed with the Constitutional Court by losing 2024 presidential candidates Ganjar Pranowo and Anies Baswedan. Jokowi had chosen to back his former political rival, Prabowo Subianto, when he made a third and finally successful presidential run in 2024 after choosing Jokowi's eldest son, Gibran Rakabuming Raka, as his vice-presidential running mate. The losing candidates charged the Jokowi administration with misappropriating state resources, including social assistance, 'to sway voters in favour of the Prabowo-Gibran pair as part of his attempt to maintain his grip on power after leaving office later this year' (Indra, 2024).

This use of social assistance as patronage in Indonesia has to be seen against the backdrop of the country spending just a little over 1 per cent of its GDP on social welfare programmes (OECD, 2022). This suggests universal schemes take a back seat to particularistic use of funding for political purposes. In short, in both Indonesia and the Philippines, the major legacy of temporary increases in social assistance during the COVID-19 pandemic was not an overall increase or an institutionalisation of social welfare, but rather the creation of new sources of political patronage for presidents to use in their efforts to secure or extend their political influence.

Malaysia and Thailand: Legitimacy crisis, policy incoherence, and reconfiguration of elite power

The Malaysian and Thai cases are distinct from both the technocratic, anti-welfarist ideology of Singapore's ruling

PAP, which opposed expanding social welfare programmes beyond the pandemic, and the populist–patronage strategies of the Indonesian and Philippine presidents, which favoured increasing patronage over universal welfare strategies. Yet what all three country cases shared was strong public support for their respective governments throughout the pandemic, despite their very different levels of performance. By contrast, in Malaysia and Thailand, governments had lower levels of political legitimacy and faced major civil society protests during the pandemic.

Although both Malaysia and Thailand performed relatively well during 2020 and 2021 in terms of limiting COVID-19 excess death rates, they did considerably worse in 2022 and after (The Economist, 2024). Moreover, their economies suffered severe downturns from 2020 to 2021, behind only the Philippines. Social assistance, as elsewhere, mitigated the worst impact of the pandemic but was not enough to stem growing discontent.

Although conservative elites suffered electoral defeat in both countries, they managed to successfully reconfigure their power through coalition governments with opposition parties that largely abandoned their reformist ambitions in order to share state power. Rather than further institutionalising social welfare measures, political constituencies were catered to through one-time aid handouts or through promises of preferential treatment for a particular ethno-religious constituency in the aftermath of the pandemic.

Malaysia and Thailand are distinctive among our five Southeast Asian cases as the impact of COVID-19 on guiding government policy seemed to be secondary to the impact on coping with considerable pre-existing civil society protest against regimes widely seen as illegitimate. The 2014 military coup overthrew a government led by the sister of Thaksin Shinawatra, former prime minister and populist leader of the country's largest political party, Pheu Thai. The military junta repressed the pro-Thaksin 'red shirts' protest movement.

However, the 2019 elections – the first the military had allowed since the coup – showed the resilience of Pheu Thai and a new opposition party, Future Forward, which were only denied control of a new government through institutional manipulation. When the Future Forward Party was banned and a Thai exile activist was kidnapped and presumed killed, large student protests began in mid-2020 and continued into 2022. Pro-democracy demonstrators rallied in Bangkok and other major Thai cities in an attempt to force political change in the face of police crackdowns, defying warnings from authorities about the kingdom's rapidly rising COVID-19 cases.

In Malaysia, the reformist Pakatan Harapan coalition had won a surprise victory in the 2018 general election, ending the United Malay National Organisation's unbroken hold on power since independence in 1957. However, Pakatan Harapan was forced from power in the early 2020 by political manoeuvring known as the 'Sheraton move', since much of the strategising took place in a hotel of that name. Rather than call new elections, a new Perikatan Nasional (PN) coalition government, which excluded most of the reformists, was agreed. Although it was formed undemocratically, the coalition initially enjoyed public support during the first wave of COVID-19, as the government was seemingly focused on containing the outbreak. However, after the PN government refused to reconvene parliament and subsequently announced a state of emergency (from January to August 2021), that support declined (Panneerselvam and Tayeb, 2023).

As COVID-19 cases rose exponentially despite the clampdown, oppositionists found creative ways to circumvent pandemic restrictions in order to mount public protests and engage in online activism, and there was widespread media coverage of the pushback. The severe economic impact of these strict pandemic measures 'built up public resentment against the government and contributed to its unpopularity' (Panneerselvam and Tayeb, 2023: 423). The government's apparent failure to contain the COVID-19 pandemic and the country's growing dissatisfaction with the mounting economic controls resulted in a loss of majority support by the PN coalition. The government was forced to resign in August 2021 after just 17 months in power, and a snap general election was called in late 2022.

While both Thailand and Malaysia provided generous social assistance during the pandemic, this only partially mitigated the severe economic impact of the pandemic. Thailand suffered the region's second-sharpest economic contraction in 2020, of 6.1 per cent (with only the Philippines experiencing a worse downturn, of 9.5 per cent; Bentzen and Tung, 2024). The bottom fell out of household consumption, with it dropping from THB 1.65 trillion (USD 46 billion) in the fourth quarter of 2019 to below THB 1.4 trillion (USD 39 billion) in the second quarter of 2020 (Amphunan et al, 2022). Although the economy recovered somewhat the following year, it lagged behind most other Association of Southeast Asian Nations countries, with an overall decline of 2.3 per cent between 2020 and 2021 (World Bank Group, 2023). Thailand's economic recovery in 2021 was blunted by the emergence of new COVID-19 variants and slow progress in vaccinations, triggering strict new containment measures, which the most vulnerable in Thai society bore disproportionately (Glaser, 2021).

In spring of 2020, the Thai government drew up a pandemic relief package worth THB 2.2 trillion (USD 63 billion), or 12.9 per cent of GDP (World Bank Group, 2023: 3). This financed the additional health costs related to the pandemic, provided relief to less well off Thais, and aimed to stabilise the economy, threatened in particular by the abrupt loss of once high tourist revenue. The greatest economic impact of the pandemic was felt by low-income households, women, individuals in low education groups, and those in the south. Yet given that an estimated 44 million Thais benefited from social assistance and social insurance programmes during the pandemic, poverty only increased from 6.2 per cent in 2019 to 6.4 per cent in 2020, rather than the 7.4 per cent estimated if the compensation package was not in place (Belghith and Arayavechkit, 2021).

Of particular importance was the No One Left Behind (Rao Mai Ting Gun) temporary wage subsidy scheme targeting informal workers, who make up the majority of the labour force in Thailand but are not insured under the country's Social Security Fund. It was designed to supplement the means-tested Social Welfare Card, launched in 2017, which was designed to aid low-income Thais, the elderly, persons with disabilities, and children. These new measures, added to existing social insurance schemes, supported an estimated 42.4 million Thais, or about 60 per cent of the population. Aid was distributed through a relatively efficient mobile app system, complemented by state-owned banks (Amphunan et al, 2022).

Malaysia's economy declined by 5.5 per cent in 2020 – its worst economic performance since the 7.4 per cent contraction in 1998 during the Asian financial crisis and down from its 4.3 per cent growth in 2019 (Bentzen and Tung, 2024). Job losses were initially severe, with employees in the informal sector and women most affected. Vulnerable worker groups experienced employment losses many times higher than the average worker, and as economic recovery began, it favoured male, older, higher-educated, and more experienced workers. The impact of the first mobility control order, a nearly total lockdown, allowed only essential services to operate, but only at 50 per cent capacity, resulting in a steep 17.1 per cent decline in GDP in the second quarter, with job losses reaching nearly a million by May 2020 (Federation of Malaysian Manufacturers, 2021).

During mid-2021, the Malaysian government introduced eight major pandemic relief measures – totalling over MYR 850 billion (USD 191 billion) – to ease economic hardship and to limit economic decline (Purnamasari and Ahmad, 2021). Initially termed Generating, Caring, Loving, and Empowering (Penjana, Prihatin, Permai, and Permekasa), this relief programme was wide-ranging. It included cash payments to the bottom 40 per cent of households and particularly affected groups (such as workers, farmers, fishers, pensioners, and those working in the tourist sector), special allowances for healthcare workers and other 'frontliners' (police, immigration workers, customs workers, and so on), free internet at the height of the pandemic, rent exemptions for public housing for several months, subsidies for small and medium-sized enterprises and micro-enterprises, and wage subsidies for affected businesses. By mid-2021, nearly 60 per cent of households had received government assistance, including cash transfers, moratoria on loan repayments, and tax relief. Yet, due to bureaucratic inefficiency with weak targeting and delivery of aid, many poorer Malaysians had still not received any assistance despite the strict lockdown, which sometimes led to severe food insecurity and large drops in income (Purnamasari and Ahmad, 2021). Also, the impact of large-scale disbursements in Malaysia was blunted by 'high living costs, sluggish growth, and low saving rates among the population even pre-pandemic' (Amul et al, 2022: 99). As of November 2021, these government relief packages represented about 43.5 per cent of GDP, increasing the Malaysian central government's debt from 52.4 per cent of GDP in 2019 to 60.4 per cent in 2022 (International Monetary Fund, 2023).

In Thailand and Malaysia, the pandemic response largely involved building on existing forms of social expenditure at a time when governments were suffering from severe legitimacy crises and were primarily occupied with staying in power as civil society pushback mounted. In Thailand, the student protests from 2020 to 2022 were not initially linked to the pandemic, but the government's fumbling response to it fuelled further demonstrations. This seemed to absorb much of the government's energies, leading to a lack of policy coherence that contributed to higher excess death rates. Glaser (2021) argues there is a need to differentiate 'between a rather successful attempt to deal with the pandemic at the outset and a later increasingly disappointing attempt' involving a flawed vaccine rollout, including a high-level scandal about vaccine development and procurement, as well as a bad third wave of COVID-19. Given its political preoccupations, the government relied largely on supplementing existing welfare schemes, as discussed earlier, although these were not sufficient to stop an economic downturn in 2020.

With the Thai government's legitimacy crisis worsened due to its flawed pandemic response, it is not surprising that the May 2023 election was dominated by the two opposition parties: the Move Forward Party – the successor to the Future Forward Party, which had close links to the student protest movement – and Pheu Thai – the party of former Prime Minister Thaksin. The two pro-military parties representing the military junta, which had reigned openly from 2014 to 2019 and behind the scenes since then, were badly defeated. Yet, a new constitution was 'ratified' after the coup, with a conservative Constitutional Court and an appointed senate as major institutional instruments, and the Move Forward Party was prevented from forming a government (and was later banned by the Constitutional Court). Pheu Thai then formed an uneasy alliance with one of the military parties, the United Thai Nation Party. With the 'military-monarchical regime' still intact behind the façade of this civilian government, there was little change in Thai politics between the pre- and post-pandemic periods.

Levels of social welfare in Thailand soon returned to their pre-pandemic levels. Thailand spent only 3.7 per cent of GDP on social protection in 2015, although this amount had increased in the run-up to the 2019 election (OECD, 2022). Also, access to social welfare funding had improved somewhat due to digitisation undertaken during COVID-19. Yet inequality continued to worsen during the pandemic. In 2021, Thailand registered an income Gini coefficient of 43.3 per cent, the highest in not only Southeast Asia but also the entire Asia Pacific region, making it one of the most unequal countries globally (World Bank Group, 2023: vii). Consumer confidence also remained significantly below 2019 levels, with post-COVID-19 inflationary pressures dampening household spending.

During the pandemic, under the unelected and unpopular PN coalition government, Malaysia became 'both poorer and more unequal', with 'inadequate social protection for the most vulnerable' meaning 'that the employment impacts of the COVID-19 crisis have had enormous effects on household incomes', which fell by 11.3 per cent in 2020 (Cheng, 2022). General elections were called early in 2022 to deal with an ongoing legitimacy crisis in which three governments had fallen in two years. But the election results were ambiguous, with the opposition Pakatan Harapan winning a plurality of seats but only able to form a government by working with former authoritarian ruling party the United Malay National Organisation. Although led by long-time oppositionist Anwar Ibrahim, the coalition government was unable or unwilling to follow through on opposition promises of democratic reform and good governance. Acutely aware of the coalition's dwindling support among Malay voters, the government increased the budget for the Department of Islamic Development and allowed the remit of Sharia courts to be expanded. At the same time, in the name of fiscal responsibility, the Anwar-led government did not significantly increase funding for universal welfare measures. Rather than launching new policy initiatives, including an expansion of welfare protections, a reconfigured conservative elite fell back into its religiously oriented, fiscally conservative grooves. In a country not strongly inclined towards welfare programmes or social safety nets, the increase in COVID-19 social protection spending was seen as a temporary lapse requiring fiscal correction.

Conclusion

This chapter has analysed the institutional factors which are a major factor explaining why there were only meagre longer-term increases in the provision of social welfare support despite the enormous impact of the pandemic. It has been shown how the dominance of conservative elites quickly reoriented the political and policy directions of these states back to an approximation of pre-pandemic normalcy in terms of welfare spending. This was achieved due the marginalisation or co-optation of oppositional forces, which had often been weakened by backsliding regimes. This left few active 'change agents' available to push for greater social inclusion after the short-term pandemic measures expired. This allowed particular institutional arrangements across the five country cases to inhibit long-term policy transformation largely unimpeded.

In Singapore, the ruling PAP government was able to enhance its technocratic image through relatively strong pandemic and economic performance while quickly rolling back social assistance measures and reaffirming its conservative neoliberal ideology. In Indonesia and the Philippines, social assistance measures undertaken during the pandemic were seen as a convenient way to ramp up patronage in the aftermath of the crisis rather than to finance an increase in universal welfare measures. Finally, in Malaysia and Thailand, conservative elites facing legitimation crises were focused on preserving their political hegemony through coalition governments, which failed to push for substantive social reforms.

Thus, social assistance, ramped up considerably to deal with pandemic dislocations, has not led to enduring welfare improvements in the five Southeast Asian countries we studied. These findings challenge the underlying assumption in historical institutional logics that critical junctures lead to change. Instead, our analysis demonstrates how the antecedent and precedent conditions can maintain institutional stability even during a crisis that threatens to overwhelm state capacity to function.

FIVE

Outcomes and implications

The COVID-19 pandemic began at the end of two decades of increased disease emergences. From severe acute respiratory syndrome (known as SARS) to bird flu to swine flu to Middle East Respiratory System (known as MERS), the global community was challenged by successive outbreaks of novel infectious diseases. None of these had the same impact as the COVID-19 pandemic, however. It proved to be a systemic shock at the international level that reverberated down through states, societies, and economies. By any measure, the pandemic opened a critical juncture – a fluid moment in time when responses to the challenges posed by the virus irrevocably changed the relationship between institutions and societies and opened the possibility of regimes taking new institutional pathways. But, at least in the five Southeast Asian countries analysed in this study, this did not occur when it came to continuing with the greater provision of social welfare, which happened briefly during the pandemic. The question, which we are now in a better position to answer, is why?

While previous shorter-term infectious disease outbreaks in the region did sensitise these states to the necessity of infectious disease response strategies, our research found that despite the huge impact of COVID-19 on these Southeast Asian societies, long-term structural factors and context-specific political dynamics precluded an institutional response that led to fundamental change in social policy. As such, despite the important differences we detailed between the cases, all Southeast Asian governments analysed in this study sought to return to quite limited welfare provision of the status quo ante. Their largely unchallenged ability to do so – despite our original survey showing that public opinion in these countries favoured more inclusive welfare measures being continued after the pandemic – reinforced notions of institutional stability and longevity. In short, rather than the critical juncture caused by the pandemic leading policy makers to embed social welfare policy reforms, it proved to be a 'negative case' in which existing institutions instead demonstrated their 'stickiness' – that is, their resistance to change.

In this concluding chapter, we synthesise the findings of the study and discuss their implications. We begin with a summary and further discussion of the results, then move on to a comparative analysis of developments in Southeast Asia and other regions in which we assess the specificity of Southeast Asia and comment on the prospects for the emergence of more comprehensive and inclusive welfare states in the region. Finally, we briefly assess long-term prospects for social policy development in Southeast Asia.

Key findings

Our analysis is based on the premise that crises – such as pandemics – can be understood as critical junctures that may alter policy trajectories and open potentially new pathways. We highlighted key aspects of a well-developed literature that has repeatedly identified conditions in which endogenous or exogenous shocks have redirected a country's path dependency, although we also noted theorisation of 'negative cases' in which such a transformation did not occur during a critical juncture. From this perspective, our study of COVID-19 in Southeast Asia delivers five important findings.

The first is that, as hypothesised, the COVID-19 pandemic can indeed be conceptualised as a disruptive event which may fundamentally change how people think about important policy issues. In the five country cases analysed in this book, we found significant evidence supporting an attitudinal change argument, as many of the respondents we surveyed reported having changed their social policy preferences as a result of the pandemic. To be sure, there are significant differences in attitudinal change across the five samples we studied, with Singaporeans showing the least desire for greater social policy measures. Yet our analysis also indicates that perceptions of attitudinal change are common in all countries. Thus, the conclusion that we can draw based on the Southeast Asian experience is that, from a public opinion perspective, COVID-19 has been transformational in terms of strengthening support for more socially inclusive policies. A question which remains to be investigated is whether the attitudinal changes we identified are short-lived or will persist for the longer term. Further studies adopting more sophisticated methodologies, such as panel analysis of more highly representative samples, may help to address this question.

Our second finding is that despite an overall shift in all countries towards favouring greater social provision, substantial variation remains to be explained within each country, across the thousands of individuals we surveyed. Specifically, in Chapter 3 we analysed a wide range of factors – from sociodemographic traits to political preferences, ideological orientations, and feelings of vulnerability – as drivers of change. This analysis allowed us to explain why some Southeast Asian citizens have changed their opinions and behaviours as a result of the pandemic, while others have not. Of particular interest here are our results on the drivers of attitudinal change, since they indicate that there is a highly complex cognitive process at play. Like behavioural change, changes in attitudes are predicted by personal exposure and risk perception, but they are also significantly influenced by ideological factors, assessments of institutional performance, trust in institutions, and even feelings of national attachment. This suggests a reason why many individuals, even if concerned with the epidemiological dimension of the pandemic, may fail to alter their beliefs about social policy. Such individuals may learn new things about the pandemic, become aware of inequalities that they did not know about previously, understand new reasons why health policies may be inadequate, and so forth. But the process through which this new information translates into demand for more comprehensive social policies is ultimately contingent on a person's pre-existing political and ideological preferences. This shows us how the barriers to adopting more inclusive social policies are not only institutional but also rooted in individual-level cognitive processes.

Third, we find that attitudinal and behavioural change does not necessarily lead to policy change due to intervening 'sticky' institutional factors. In the five countries included in this study, there appears to be a major disconnect between how ordinary people and government institutions have responded to the pandemic. Many citizens appear to have developed new understandings and preferences following the disruptions of the pandemic, suggesting that a demand for policy change in the realm of social policy is indeed present, as we initially hypothesised. As shown in Chapter 4, despite the highly varied response of institutions in these Southeast Asia cases, all have led to continuity with current policies and practices instead of leading to significant policy change regarding social policy. Welfare state institutions in the region have largely kept their conservative, minimalist profile. Today, they look quite similar to what they were like before the pandemic, and there are no clear prospects for change in the near future. To be sure, it would be naive to assume an automatic link between public opinion and policy change, as government responsiveness is a complex process that is mediated by various political and institutional factors (Schnose, 2015). Yet, the disjunction observed here raises important questions about the mechanisms that shape policy responsiveness in Southeast Asia and elsewhere. It reminds us of the importance of jointly examining the demand and supply side of policy change, and to be aware of the complex interplay between public opinion, institutional structures, and policy development.

Related to this, our fourth finding sheds light on what factors may explain the discrepancy between micro-level and macro-level patterns of change, and specifically on what institutional factors may have hindered the adoption of more comprehensive social policies. To address this aspect, our starting point was to acknowledge the importance of the repression of Leftist forces and progressive civil society actors across the region. Thus, potential 'change agents' who could have pushed for the translation of citizens' changed preferences into more inclusive social policies were generally weakened or missing altogether. Beyond these unfavourable 'permissive' conditions, the diversity of the political and institutional landscape of Southeast Asia also proved to be a decisive limitation. A variety of factors were analysed, such as the predominance of neoliberal, anti-welfarist ideologies to justify the retrenchment of social assistance, the expansion of patronage networks rather than greater expenditure on universal welfare schemes, and conservative elites with weak legitimation and a poor pandemic response successfully co-opting opposition parties while reducing social provision in the name of fiscal responsibility.

The fifth key finding worth emphasising is the significant role of political legitimacy in shaping responses to the pandemic, a pattern evident both in our micro-level and our macro-level analyses. At the individual level, trust emerges as a highly significant and robust predictor of increased support for more generous social policies, and notably it is one of the few factors whose effect is consistent across all five countries. As we discussed, this is likely because individuals who perceive their government as legitimate are more inclined to trust it with taking on new functions and responsibilities. While the role of trust in fostering good governance is well documented, our findings suggest that perceptions of legitimacy are vital not only for making existing policies work, but also for enabling transitions to new policy frameworks, such as larger, more inclusive welfare states. At the institutional level, we have observed the challenges faced by countries experiencing legitimacy crises, such as Malaysia and Thailand. In low-legitimacy contexts, moving towards comprehensive welfare policies is not just ideologically contentious – it is also problematic in a deeper, more structural sense, as weak legitimacy may undermine processes of institution building and policy reform. The development of welfare policies is thus constrained by factors such as institutional capacity, regime type, and level of socioeconomic development, but also by public views of institutional legitimacy.

Together, these findings highlight an under-explored linkage between institutions and public opinions in the critical junctures literature (Shim, 2024: 96–97). If institutions are to successfully navigate the challenges posed by a critical juncture, then they need public support to legitimate their authority and adhere to any new policies deployed; hence the significance of institutional and social trust. However, as our research shows, public support for institutions does not automatically translate into the promulgation of policies within the critical juncture period that are responsive to public concerns. Depending on the severity of the challenge posed by the crisis, such policies may instead be directed towards strengthening the regime and its institutions – a finding echoed by Bates et al (2024).

This study's findings of the existence of such a 'negative' relationship suggests that the relationship between institutions and public opinions needs to be more carefully unpacked to explain the outcomes arising from critical junctures. Reconsidering the degree of alignment between an institutional drive for policy change and the public support for such a response serves to disaggregate the extent of new path dependencies and creates an evaluative mechanism for how impactful the critical juncture was for the regime and its society. In recognition of this need, rather than looking for a one-size-fits-all explanation, we have delved into the nuanced political context of the five countries we studied and identified various factors to account for the lack of policy change. By highlighting these diverse political and institutional landscapes, we argue that the gap between public attitudes and policy outcomes should not be attributed to a single overarching factor, but rather to a confluence of longer-term structural and shorter-term contextual variables. This finding underscores the importance of comparative research that accounts for both commonalities and divergences across cases, in Southeast Asia and beyond.

Southeast Asia in comparative perspective

When we discussed our choice of Southeast Asia as the empirical focus of this book in the introductory chapter, we argued that this region offers significant contrasts to the Western cases that dominate existing studies on the COVID-19 pandemic. First, Southeast Asia is exceptionally diverse in terms of countries' political institutions, level of socioeconomic development, and cultural and historical context. Second, to the extent that commonalities can be identified across the region, its overall trajectory of economic development and welfare state formation differs markedly from the European experience, having been heavily shaped by authoritarian legacies, conservative ideologies, the absence or suppression of Leftist parties, often severe constraints on civil society, and a focus on economic growth over redistribution. These specificities, well known to scholars of the region, represent a distinctive set of initial conditions under which a crisis like COVID-19 unfolds, creating dynamics that could be quite different from those in Western contexts.

However, the fact that Southeast Asia's initial conditions differ from those in the West does not imply a deterministic argument in which outcomes are predetermined to diverge.

As demonstrated in this book, individual- and macro-level mediating factors play a crucial role in shaping how crises may translate into policy changes or the lack thereof, which highlights the importance of context and contingencies in understanding crisis responses. In the following brief discussion, we turn to the comparative literature to explore the extent to which the findings reported here resonate with those of similar inquiries conducted in other regions. By engaging with these broader debates, we aim to situate our study, and the experience of Southeast Asia, within a global conversation on the role of COVID-19 and, more broadly, similar crises.

Our findings reveal that attitudinal change in Southeast Asia is both significant and concentrated in specific segments of the population. While a substantial portion of our Southeast Asian respondents remained supportive of the limited, conservative welfare state regimes characteristic of the region, most individuals surveyed expressed increased support for a larger role of the state in social policy. This pattern contrasts with findings from countries with more established and comprehensive welfare states, where the pandemic appears to have induced less significant shifts in public attitudes. For instance, Ebbinghaus et al (2022), using longitudinal survey data from Germany, demonstrated that most respondents maintained their support for the country's already popular generous social programmes, with only a temporary increase in support among more sceptical segments of the population. Similar findings emerge from data on South Korea and the United Kingdom, where limited increases in support for more expansive social policies have been attributed to the relatively limited impact of COVID-19 or to perceptions of the pandemic as an exceptional and transitory event (De Vries et al, 2023; Kim, 2024). Further, survey experiments in Western Europe suggest that the economic anxieties triggered by the pandemic may have had a short-term dampening effect on support for increased social spending, at least during the very initial phase of the crisis (Daniele et al, 2020).

In summary, then, research from these developed countries indicates less pronounced shifts in public opinion than those we observed in Southeast Asia. One factor that could explain these findings is that developed economies, with their greater resources and higher state capacity, were better equipped to manage the pandemic's economic and social disruptions. This explanation aligns with our data, as the country in our study that exhibited the least attitudinal change, Singapore, is also the wealthiest and most developed in the region. Yet the divergence may also stem from the more expansive welfare institutions already established in many European cases. In countries with well-developed welfare states, the baseline level of support for social policy may leave less room for additional shifts in public attitudes. In such contexts, because of policy feedback mechanisms that strengthen support for existing welfare state arrangements, citizens may have already developed positive attitudes towards broad-based social policies, making significant increases in support less likely even in the wake of a disruptive crisis. In this respect, Southeast Asia's experience may resemble that of low- and middle-income countries in the Global South more than that of advanced Western economies.

When we focus on the determinants of attitudinal change, our findings for Southeast Asia are reminiscent of those emerging from the comparative literature. Trust, in its various forms, is one of the most widely analysed variables, with numerous studies identifying it as a powerful mediator of attitudinal and behavioural responses to the pandemic (Devine et al, 2021). Research from Western contexts has also highlighted the significant role of partisan polarisation in shaping pandemic-related attitudes, as evidenced in the United States (Gadarian et al, 2021) and Western Europe (Altiparmakis et al, 2021). Although partisan inclinations do not show a significant direct effect in most of our models for Southeast Asia, these insights from the comparative literature resonate with our finding that evaluations of government performance play a critical role, as these assessments are typically endogenous to partisan dynamics. Ideology also appears to influence how individuals and political actors conceptualise and respond to the pandemic, as seen in research on political elites in Australia, for example (Petter and Howard, 2024). Additionally, similar to findings from our study, research suggests that experiences of the pandemic, and economic disruptions especially, shape increased support for social spending, although these effects are often more pronounced within specific population groups (Tonelli et al, 2024). Lastly, a large cross-country study demonstrated that attachment to national identity correlates with higher support for public health initiatives and preventive behaviours (Van Bavel et al, 2022). While macro-level factors such as state capacity and institutional frameworks undeniably influenced the pandemic's trajectory, a focus on individual-level dynamics reveals important similarities across regions, highlighting the universality of certain mediating factors in shaping attitudinal and behavioural change following a major crisis.

Moving to macro-level policy change, developments in Southeast Asia in some respects mirror those observed in advanced economies, despite the marked differences in socioeconomic development and welfare state institutions at the onset of the pandemic. First, the short-term responses by Southeast Asian governments, which included vigorous initiatives such as significant deficit spending and large-scale temporary social protection programmes, were not unique to the region, as similar measures were widely implemented across advanced economies (Moreira and Hick, 2021). These parallels reflect a recurrent, quasi-automatic policy response to counter the worst of the pandemic's socioeconomic fallout, even if less developed economies have typically implemented more limited interventions due to resource constraints (Dorlach, 2023). Second, existing studies addressing the key question of whether crises like COVID-19 can catalyse long-term changes in social policy and foster more inclusive institutions offer insights consistent with our findings. As we observed in Southeast Asia, these studies suggest that there has been little evidence of a general policy shift in this direction. While it may be too early to make definitive conclusions, much of the evidence points to continuity as a more common outcome than transformative change (Béland et al, 2021a).

Comparative research, however, identifies greater variation across countries in policy institutionalisation than we observed within Southeast Asia (Cruz-Martínez et al, 2023). There are, of course, numerous factors that may account for this variation. For instance, the predominance of anti-welfarist ideology has been highlighted as crucial in shaping outcomes in Britain, although significant attitudinal shifts can occur even in countries where such ideologies are dominant (Orton and Sarkar, 2023). However, most analyses of cross-country variation emphasise the pivotal role of policy legacies and pre-existing welfare institutions. For example, some scholars have noted that Nordic welfare states were strengthened, relying on their robust existing frameworks to adapt and expand (Greve et al, 2021). Similarly, continental European countries such as Germany, Belgium, and the Netherlands enhanced their social policies, often building on established insurance-based schemes (Cantillon et al, 2021). Even among countries with similar welfare state models, such as Canada and the United States, policy legacies shaped divergent trajectories, illustrating once again the crucial role of extant policy trajectories in mediating crisis response (Béland et al, 2021b). This strong historical institutionalist emphasis in comparative research aligns with the theoretical approach we adopted in our study of Southeast Asia. When we extend our analysis beyond the region, the broader variation in welfare state institutions helps us to understand how the distinct historical trajectories of welfare state development in Southeast Asia have constrained progressive policy change in the wake of the COVID-19 pandemic.

Final thoughts

Throughout this book, we have leveraged the COVID-19 pandemic as a case study of how large-scale crises may be able to catalyse change across individuals and institutions. Crises are often theorised as being critical junctures with the potential to disrupt entrenched structures and foster innovation, and we have argued that COVID-19 can be fruitfully conceptualised as such a momentous development. Yet, the evidence from our analysis in Southeast Asia, as well as from studies in other regions, suggests that the transformative role of crises may be more constrained than often previously thought. Short-term adaptations during the pandemic, such as the rapid expansion of social safety nets and emergency healthcare measures, were common and impressive in the scale and speed of their deployment. However, these measures have rarely translated into long-term institutional reforms. While we have shown that in the case of five Southeast Asian countries there was a notable shift in public attitudes towards more inclusive welfare policies, this differed from many more economically developed settings where pre-existing comprehensive welfare frameworks mitigated demands for more extensive social provision.

This raises the question as to whether or not the limited transformative impact in the COVID-19 case is unique to this crisis or may extend to crises more generally. Perhaps the relatively short-lived nature of crises like a pandemic may explain the lack of sustained political and social momentum necessary for enduring change. Yet, the dramatic impact of COVID-19 and the scale and depth of the disruptions occurring in such a short time frame could also be seen as ideal to foster change given the compelling sense of urgency they generated. Ultimately, the lessons of COVID-19 highlight that while crises can disrupt the status quo, the degree to which they facilitate systemic change depends on contextual factors, particularly the silencing or sidelining of potential agents of change and the ability of regimes to employ strategies which co-opt, redirect, or suppress potential pressures for institutional transformation.

The pandemic has also underscored the limitations of welfare state institutions in Southeast Asia by exposing significant inequalities in social protection. Based on our analysis, while the pandemic did prompt temporary expansions in various social policy programmes across the region, barriers to more expansive and inclusive welfare states have remained strong as these Southeast Asian regimes do not appear to have questioned their reliance on conservative, productivist models of welfare provision. We have argued that the earlier repression of Leftist political forces, the marginalisation of civil society, and the various institutional stratagems explain the lack of sustained expansion of social provision after the pandemic subsided. This raises an important question about the prospects of welfare state development in the region. We sometimes think of the development of inclusive welfare systems as resulting both from significant state capacity made available through socioeconomic modernisation and institution building and from strong advocacy by progressive political actors. While many countries in Southeast Asia are increasingly satisfying the former requirement, the latter remains elusive because of historical authoritarian suppression of Leftist parties, weak labour movements, democratic backsliding – which has often weakened civil society – conservative economic ideologies, the prevalence of clientelistic linkages, ethnic-based politics, and opportunistic coalitions. Can Southeast Asian welfare state institutions, then, transition towards a more encompassing framework despite such deep-seated constraints?

The path towards more expansive welfare states in the region seems uncertain and protracted. Based on the experience of advanced economies, one could speculate that this path would likely require a sustained and widespread process of attitudinal change, surpassing the shifts we observed in our study; this latent demand for more equitable social policies would need to coalesce into a coherent programmatic agenda, gain traction through social and political mobilisation, and eventually incentivise political elites to prioritise these demands. Our analysis of the COVID-19 experience in Southeast Asia suggests that these conditions are not yet present and that the likelihood of immediate change remains low.

But adopting this perspective might reflect an overly Eurocentric view of welfare state development, and the assumption that welfare state expansion is necessarily associated with progressive movements may be unwarranted. After all, even in Europe, conservative parties have historically played a crucial role in expanding welfare state institutions, and sometimes social protection policies have even had authoritarian origins, such as the social insurance schemes introduced under Bismarck's Germany. Similarly, Southeast Asia may forge its own unique path towards more inclusive social policies – one that does not necessarily follow the European model or require embracing explicitly welfarist ideologies. If such conservative or even authoritarian-led institutionalisation of expanded social protection does come about one day, the region may ultimately serve as a policy laboratory for innovative solutions in non-Western contexts.

Appendix: Sociodemographic composition of the five samples

TOWARDS INCLUSIVE SOCIAL POLICIES?

		Indonesia	Malaysia	Philippines	Singapore	Thailand
Age	Median age	38	46	34	45	42
Gender	Male	50%	49%	50%	51%	49%
	Female	50%	51%	50%	49%	51%
Education	College educated	59%	39%	58%	41%	45%
	Non-college educated	41%	61%	42%	59%	55%
Income	Basic needs only	26%	36%	44%	37%	28%
	Can save small amount	28%	26%	24%	32%	24%
	Financially secure	15%	13%	6%	18%	8%
	Struggles to make ends meet	31%	24%	27%	13%	40%
Religion	Buddhist	2%	35%	0%	32%	90%
	Christian/Catholic	18%	21%	90%	28%	3%
	Hindu	1%	4%	0%	4%	0%
	Muslim	77%	34%	2%	16%	5%
	None	0%	4%	2%	17%	2%
	Other	0%	2%	6%	2%	0%

APPENDIX

		Indonesia	Malaysia	Philippines	Singapore	Thailand
Region	Sumatra	23%				
	Java	60%				
	Kalimantan	5%				
	Sulawesi	5%				
	Papua	1%				
	Other	6%				
	Peninsular Malaysia		79%			
	Sabah		8%			
	Sarawak		11%			
	Other		2%			
	Luzon			65%		
	Visayas			16%		
	Mindanao			18%		
	Other			1%		
	North				25%	
	South				2%	

(continued)

	Indonesia	Malaysia	Philippines	Singapore	Thailand
East				25%	
West				24%	
Central				24%	
North					21%
Northeast					21%
Central					41%
South					13%
Other					4%

Note: Some categories do not sum to 100% due to rounding.

Notes

one
[1] Five other regimes were excluded because they lack a significant electoral component – Brunei, Laos, and Vietnam (Croissant and Lorenz, 2018) – or no longer have one – Cambodia (Morgenbesser, 2019) and Myanmar since the 2021 coup. Although Timor-Leste does have a significant electoral component and has overcome recent democratic setbacks (Feijó, 2023), it was not possible to include it due to technical, research-related factors.

three
[1] The first group comprised of a bigger role of government in healthcare, protection against sickness and accidents, protection against job loss, better childcare services, and protection from poverty. The second group comprised of better training to improve workers' skills, universal basic income, reduction of inequality, a bigger role of the state in the economy, and economic redistribution. For each group, the average scores were calculated, and those with a score of 4 or higher were categorised as reporting a high level of attitudinal change.

[2] The former group includes respondents who need help to meet their monthly expenses or can barely make it on their own, while the latter includes respondents who are able to save some money every month and those who are financially secure.

[3] In order to explain differences in attitudinal change in terms of social class and gender that run contrary to existing theoretical expectations, new hypotheses on the impact of demographic factors would need to be developed. However, this is beyond the scope of this book.

[4] Indeed, the two indicators are correlated, as the mean value of our trust index increased from 5.5 among those who reported they do not feel very close or not close at all to their nation to 6.6 among those who said they feel somewhat close and 7.5 among those who said they feel very close to their nation.

References

Acemoglu, D. and Robinson, J. 2023. Weak, despotic, or inclusive? How state type emerges from state versus civil society competition. *American Political Science Review*, 117(2): 407–420.

Agley, J., Xiao, Y., Thompson, E.E., Chen, X. and Golzarri-Arroyo, L. 2021. Intervening on trust in science to reduce belief in COVID-19 misinformation and increase COVID-19 preventive behavioral intentions: randomized controlled trial. *Journal of Medical Internet Research*, 23(10): art e32425, https://doi.org/10.2196/32425

Albarracin, D. and Shavitt, S. 2018. Attitudes and attitude change. *Annual Review of Psychology*, 69(1): 299–327.

Allan, J. and Scruggs, L. 2004. Political partisanship and welfare state reform in advanced industrial societies. *American Journal of Political Science*, 48(3): 496–512.

Altiparmakis, A., Bojar, A., Brouard, S., Foucault, M., Kriesi, H. and Nadeau, R. 2021. Pandemic politics: policy evaluations of government responses to COVID-19. *West European Politics*, 44(5–6): 1159–1179.

Amphunan, K., Zhang, K. and Banu, F. 2022. Booster shot? Pao Tang digital payment and Thailand's domestic consumption. *Fulcrum* (12 July), https://fulcrum.sg/booster-shot-pao-tang-digital-payment-and-thailands-domestic-consumption

Amrith, S. 2014. The internationalization of health in Southeast Asia. In T. Harper and S. Amrith (eds), *Histories of Health in Southeast Asia: Perspectives on the Long Twentieth Century*. Indiana University Press, 161–179.

REFERENCES

Amul, G., Ang, M., Kraybill, D., Ong, S.E. and Yoong, J. 2022. Responses to COVID-19 in Southeast Asia: diverse paths and ongoing challenges. *Asian Economic Policy Review*, 17: 90–110.

An, B. and Tang, S. 2020. Lessons from COVID-19 responses in East Asia: institutional infrastructure and enduring policy instruments. *American Review of Public Administration*, 50(6–7): 790–800.

Androff, D. and Abbas, S. 2023. Social protection responses to COVID-19 in Indonesia. In L. Patel, S. Plagerson, and I. Chinyoka (eds), *Handbook on Social Protection and Social Development in the Global South*. Elgar Press, 486–499.

Arguelles, C.V. 2021. The populist brand is crisis: curable Dutertismo amidst mismanaged COVID-19 response. In D. Singh and M. Cook (eds), *Southeast Asian Affairs 2021*. ISEAS–Yusof Ishak Institute, 257–274.

Arguelles, C. 2022. The triumph of the Marcos-Duterte leviathan. *The Medium* (10 May), https://medium.com/@clevearguelles/the-triumph-of-the-marcos-duterteleviathan-f8b8165b9759

Arugay, A.A. and Baquisal, J.K.A. 2023. Bowed, bent, & broken: Duterte's assaults on civil society in the Philippines. *Journal of Current Southeast Asian Affairs*, 42(3), 328–349.

ASEAN (Association of Southeast Asian Nations). 2020. *ASEAN Rapid Assessment: The Impact of COVID-19 on Livelihoods across ASEAN*. ASEAN Secretariat, https://asean.org/wp-content/uploads/2021/08/ASEAN-Rapid-Assessment_Final-23112020.pdf

ASEAN BioDiaspora Virtual Center. 2023. *COVID-19 and Mpox: Situational Report in the ASEAN Region*, ASEAN, 13 March, https://asean.org/wp-content/uploads/2023/03/COVID-19-and-Mpox_Situational-Report_ASEAN-BioDiaspora-Regional-Virtual-Center_13Mar2023.pdf

Asian Development Bank. 2020. *Social Amelioration Guidelines* (13 April), www.adb.org/sites/default/files/linked-documents/43407-017-sd-05.pdf

Aslam, M. and Gunaratna, R. 2022. *COVID-19 in South, West, and Southeast Asia: Risk and Response in the Early Phase*. Routledge.

Aspalter, C. 2006. The East Asian welfare model. *International Journal of Social Welfare*, 15(4): 290–301.

Aspinall, E. 2015. Money politics: patronage and clientelism in Southeast Asia. In W. Case (ed), *Routledge Handbook of Southeast Asian Democratization*. Routledge, 299–313.

Aspinall, E., Curato, N., Fossati, D., Warburton, E. and Weiss, M.L. 2021. *COVID-19 in Southeast Asia: Public Health, Social Impacts, and Political Attitudes*, SEARBO Policy Briefing (August). New Madala, www.newmandala.org/wp-content/uploads/2021/08/SEARBO_COVID-19-in-Southeast-Asia_Public-health-social-impacts-and-political-attitudes_final.pdf

Aspinall, E., Weiss, M.L., Hicken, A. and Hutchcroft, P.D. 2022. *Mobilizing for Elections: Patronage and Political Machines in Southeast Asia*. Cambridge University Press.

Ayalon, L. 2021. Trust and compliance with COVID-19 preventive behaviors during the pandemic. *International Journal of Environmental Research and Public Health*, 18(5): art 2643, https://doi.org/10.3390/ijerph18052643

Baldwin, P. 1990. *The Politics of Social Solidarity: Class Bases of the European Welfare State 1875–1975*. Cambridge University Press.

Banks, N. and Hulme, D. 2012. The role of NGOs and civil society in development and poverty reduction. *Brooks World Poverty Institute Working Paper*, (171), https://papers.ssrn.com/sol3/papers.cfm?abstract_id=2072157

Basilio, J., Britt-Fermo, L. and Cacnio, F.C.Q. 2022. *Quantifying the Macroeconomic Impact of the Philippine Fiscal and Monetary Responses to the Covid-19 Pandemic*. BSP Discussion Paper 14, www.bsp.gov.ph/Pages/MediaAndResearch/PublicationsAndReports/Discussion%20Papers/DP202205.pdf

Bates, G., Barnfield, A., Pearce, N. and Ayres, S. 2024. Why didn't the 'critical juncture' of the COVID-19 pandemic lead to the reintegration of public health into urban development policy in England? *Cities & Health*, https://doi.org/10.1080/23748834.2024.2442840

Béland, D., Cantillion, B., Hick, R. and Moreira, A. 2021a. Social policy in the face of a global pandemic: policy responses to the COVID-19 crisis. *Social Policy & Administration*, 55(2): 249–260.

REFERENCES

Béland, D., Dinan, S., Rocco, P. and Waddan, L. 2021b. Social policy responses to COVID-19 in Canada and the United States: explaining policy variations between two liberal welfare state regimes. *Social Policy & Administration*, 55(2): 280–294.

Belghith, N. and Arayavechkit, T. 2021. Impact of COVID-19 on Thailand's households – insights from a rapid phone survey. *World Bank Blogs* (29 November), https://blogs.worldbank.org/en/eastasiapacific/impact-covid-19-thailands-households-insights-rapid-phone-survey

Bentzen, J. and Tung, L. 2024. Estimating the size of GDP loss in Southeast Asia due to the COVID-19 pandemic. *Eurasian Geography and Economics*, https://doi.org/0.1080/15387216.2024.2316630

Berenschot, W. 2023. Indonesia's increasingly opposition-less democracy. *East Asia Forum* (16 December), https://eastasiaforum.org/2023/12/16/indonesias-increasingly-opposition-less-democracy

Bish, A. and Michie, S. 2010. Demographic and attitudinal determinants of protective behaviours during a pandemic: a review. *British Journal of Health Psychology*, 15(4): 797–824.

Blunt, P., Turner, M. and Lindroth, H. 2012. Patronage, service delivery, and social justice in Indonesia. *International Journal of Public Administration*, 35(3): 214–220.

Boettke, P., Coyne, C.J. and Leeson, P.T. 2015. Institutional stickiness and the new development economics. In L. Grube and V. Storr (eds), *Culture and Economic Action*. Edward Elgar, 123–146.

Bordey, H. 2024. Senators question P26.7-billion aid linked to people's initiative. *GMA News* (13 February), www.gmanetwork.com/news/topstories/nation/897374/senators-question-p26-7-billion-aid-linked-to-people-s-initiative/story/#goog_rewarded

Bruine de Bruin, W. 2021. Age differences in COVID-19 risk perceptions and mental health: evidence from a national US survey conducted in March 2020. *The Journals of Gerontology: Series B*, 76(2): e24–e29.

Bünte, M. and Weiss, M. 2023. Civil society and democratic decline in Southeast Asia. *Journal of Current Southeast Asian Affairs*, 42(3): 297–307.

Campos-Castillo, C., Woodson, B.J., Theiss-Morse, E., Sacks, T., Fleig-Palmer, M.M. and Peek, M.E. 2016. Examining the relationship between interpersonal and institutional trust in political and health care contexts. In E. Shockley, T.M.S. Neal, L.M. PytlikZillig and B.H. Bornstein (eds), *Interdisciplinary Perspectives on Trust: Towards Theoretical and Methodological Integration*. Springer, 99–115.

Cantillon, B., Seeleib-Kaiser, M. and van der Veen, R. 2021. The COVID-19 crisis and policy responses by continental European welfare states. *Social Policy & Administration*, 55(2): 326–338.

Capoccia, G. 2005. *Defending Democracy: Reactions to Extremism in Interwar Europe*. Johns Hopkins University Press.

Capoccia, G. 2015. Critical junctures and institutional change. In J. Mahoney and K. Thelen (eds), *Advances in Comparative-Historical Analysis. Strategies for Social Inquiry*. Cambridge University Press, 147–179.

Capoccia, G. and Kelemen, R. 2007. The study of critical junctures: theory, narrative, and counterfactuals in historical institutionalism. *World Politics*, 59(3): 341–369.

Castillo-Carandang, N., Buenaventura, R.D., Chia, Y.C., Do Van, D., Lee, C. and Duong, N.L. 2020. Moving towards optimized noncommunicable disease management in the ASEAN region: recommendations from a review and multidisciplinary expert panel. *Risk Management and Healthcare Policy*, 13: 803–819.

Cepeda, M. 2021. Everything you need to know about the Pharmally pandemic deals scandal. *Rappler* (17 December), www.rappler.com/newsbreak/iq/list-everything-need-to-know-pharmally-covid-19-pandemic-deals-scandal

Cervantes, F. 2023. P500-B allotted for social amelioration in 2024 nat'l budget – Speaker. *Philippine News Agency* (19 December), www.pna.gov.ph/articles/1215669

Chambers, P. and Waitoolkiat, N. 2020. Faction politics in an interrupted democracy: the case of Thailand. *Journal of Current Southeast Asian Affairs*, 39(1): 144–166.

REFERENCES

Chatinakrob, T. 2020. Happiness-sharing pantries: an effective weapon to ease hunger for the needy during the pandemic in Thailand. *Swee Hock Southeast Asia Centre, LSE Blogs* (16 September), https://blogs.lse.ac.uk/seac/2020/09/16/happiness-sharing-pantries

Chen, H., Xu, W., Paris, C., Reeson, A. and Li, X. 2020. Social distance and SARS memory: impact on the public awareness of 2019 novel coronavirus (COVID-19) outbreak, *medRxiv*, https://doi.org/10.1101/2020.03.11.20033688

Cheng, C. 2022. Crisis of inequality: COVID-19's long-lasting economic impacts. *Pandemic Papers: Lessons from Covid-19*, Institute of International and Strategic Studies (2 April), www.isis.org.my/wp-content/uploads/2022/04/2-Crisis-of-inequality_Covid-19s-long-lasting-economic-impacts.pdf

Christensen, T., Lægreid, P. and Rykkja, L.H. 2016. Organizing for crisis management: building governance capacity and legitimacy. *Public Administration Review*, 76: 887–897.

Citrin, J. 1974. Comment: the political relevance of trust in government. *American Political Science Review*, 68(3): 973–988.

Coifman, K., Disabato, D.J., Aurora, P., Seah, T.H.S., Mitchell, B., Simonovic, N. et al. 2021. What drives preventive health behavior during a global pandemic? Emotion and worry. *Annals of Behavioral Medicine*, 55(8): 791–804.

Community Development Council. 2024. CDC Vouchers Scheme, www.cdc.gov.sg/our-programmes/cdcvs/#:~:text=The%20CDC%20Vouchers%20Scheme%202024,and%20help%20defray%20daily%20expenses

Croissant, A. 2004. Changing welfare regimes in East and Southeast Asia: crisis, change and challenge. *Social Policy & Administration*, 38(5): 504–524.

Croissant, A. and Lorenz, P. 2018. Government and political regimes in Southeast Asia: an introduction. In A. Croissant and P. Lorenz (eds), *Comparative Politics of Southeast Asia*. Springer, 1–20.

Cruz, C. and Keefer, P. 2015. Political parties, clientelism, and bureaucratic reform. *Comparative Political Studies*, 48(14):1942–1973.

Curato, N. 2016. Politics of anxiety, politics of hope: penal populism and Duterte's rise to power. *Journal of Current Southeast Asian Affairs*, 35(3): 91–109.

Curtice, J. 2020. Will Covid-19 change attitudes towards the welfare state? *IPPR Progressive Review*, 27(1): 93–104.

Daniele, G., Martinangeli, A., Passarelli, F., Sas, W. and Windsteiger, L. 2020. *Wind of Change? Experimental Survey Evidence on the COVID-19 Shock and Socio-Political Attitudes in Europe*. Working Paper of the Max Planck Institute for Tax Law and Public Finance No. 2020–10, https://papers.ssrn.com/sol3/papers.cfm?abstract_id=3671674

Declaration of the ASEAN Health Ministers on Collaboration on Health. 1980. Manila, 24 July, www.aseansec.org/8621.htm

Declaration of the 5th ASEAN Health Ministers Meeting on Healthy ASEAN 2020. 2000. Yogyakarta, 28–29 April, www.aseansec.org/8623.htm

Dela Cruz, A., Chu, T.-W., Lee, S.J. and Nithimasarad, C. 2022. Explaining Thailand's politicised COVID-19 containment strategies: securitisation, counter-securitisation, and re-securitisation. *Journal of Current Southeast Asian Affairs*, 41(3): 378–398.

Dellmuth, L. and Tallberg, J. 2020. Why national and international legitimacy beliefs are linked: social trust as an antecedent factor. *The Review of International Organizations*, 15: 311–337.

Devine, D., Gaskell, J., Jennings, W. and Stoker, G. 2021. Trust and the coronavirus pandemic: what are the consequences of and for trust? An early review of the literature. *Political Studies Review*, 19(2): 274–285.

De Visser, M. and Straughan, P. 2021. Singapore: technocracy and transition. In V. Ramraj (ed), *COVID-19 in Asia: Law and Policy Contexts*. Oxford University Press, 221–238.

De Vries, R., Baumberg Geiger, B., Scullion, L., Summers, K., Edmiston, D., Ingold, J. et al. 2023. Welfare attitudes in a crisis: how COVID exceptionalism undermined greater solidarity. *Journal of Social Policy*, advance online publication, https://doi.org/10.1017/S0047279423000466

REFERENCES

Dochow-Sondershaus, S. 2022. Ideological polarization during a pandemic: tracking the alignment of attitudes toward COVID containment policies and left-right self-identification. *Frontiers in Sociology*, 7, https://doi.org/10.3389/fsoc.2022.958672

Dorlach, T. 2023. Social policy responses to Covid-19 in the global south: evidence from 36 countries. *Social Policy and Society*, 22(1): 94–105.

Dulay, D., Hicken, A. and Holmes, R. 2022. The persistence of ethnopopulist support: the case of Rodrigo Duterte's Philippines. *Journal of East Asian Studies*, 22(3): 525–553.

Eadie, P. and Yacub, C. 2024. COVID-19 and aid distribution in the Philippines: a patron-clientelist explanation. *Third World Quarterly*, 45(1): 229–246.

Ebbinghaus, B., Lehner, L. and Naumann, E. 2022. Welfare state support during the COVID-19 pandemic: change and continuity in public attitudes towards social policies in Germany. *European Policy Analysis*, 8(3): 297–311.

Emmenegger, P. 2021. Agency in historical institutionalism: coalitional work in the creation, maintenance and change of institutions. *Theory & Society*, 50: 607–626.

Esmark, A. 2023. How does crisis affect the conflict between technocracy and populism? Lessons from the COVID-19 pandemic. *Politics*, 43(4): 520–535.

Esping-Andersen, G. 1990. *The Three Worlds of Welfare Capitalism*. Princeton University Press.

Falk, A., Becker, A., Dohmen, T., Huffman, D.B. and Sunde, U. 2023. The preference survey module: a validated instrument for measuring risk, time, and social preferences. *Management Science*, 69(4): 1935–1950.

Farid, M. 2019. Advocacy in action: China's grassroots NGOs as catalysts for policy innovation. *Studies in Comparative International Development*, 54(4), 528–549.

Fealy, G. 2020. Jokowi in the Covid-19 era: repressive pluralism, dynasticism and the overbearing state. *Bulletin of Indonesian Economic Studies*, 56(3): 301–323.

Federation of Malaysian Manufacturers. 2021. Federation of Malaysian Manufacturers latest to reject total lockdown as Covid-19 response, moots tougher enforcement (19 May), www.fmm.org.my/FMM_In_The_News-@-Federation_of_Malaysian_Manufacturers_latest_to_reject_total_lockdown_as_Covid-19_response,_moots_tougher_enforcement.aspx#:~:text=%E2%80%9CThe%20impact%20of%20MCO%201.0,of%20jobs%20hitting%20826%2C100%20in

Feijó, R.G. 2023. 'Elections in Timor-Leste, 2022-2023'. In R.G. Feijó (ed), *Current Electoral Processes in Southeast Asia: Regional Learnings*. HAL Open Science, hal-04304030.

Feitelson, E., Plaut, P., Salzberger, E., Shmueli, D., Altshuler, A., Amir, S. and Ben-Gal, M. 2022. Learning from others' disasters? A comparative study of SARS/MERS and COVID-19 responses in five polities. *International Journal of Disaster Risk Reduction*, 74: art 102913, https://doi.org/10.1016/j.ijdrr.2022.102913

Fenner, F. 1987. Smallpox in Southeast Asia. *Crossroads: An Interdisciplinary Journal of Southeast Asian Studies*, 3(2/3): 34–48.

Ferrara, F. 2015. *The Political Development of Thailand*. Cambridge University Press.

FitchRatings. 2025. Fitch Affirms the Philippines at 'BBB'; Outlook Stable (29 April), https://www.fitchratings.com/research/sovereigns/fitch-affirms-philippines-at-bbb-outlook-stable-29-04-2025

Flores, D. 2024. PhilHealth to run on P284 billion budget in 2025, even without gov't subsidy. *Philippine Star* (17 December), www.philstar.com/headlines/2024/12/17/2408003/philhealth-run-p284-billion-budget-2025-even-without-govt-subsidy

Foa, R., Romero-Vidal, X., Klassen, A.J., Fuenzalida Concha, J., Quednau, M. and Fenner, L.S. 2022. *The Great Reset: Public Opinion, Populism, and the Pandemic*, https://luminategroup.com/storage/1443/The_Great_Reset__Public_Opinion__Populism_and_the_Pandemic.pdf

Font, N., Graziano, P. and Tsakatika, M. 2021. Varieties of inclusionary populism? SYRIZA, Podemos and the Five Star Movement. *Government and Opposition*, 56(1): 163–183.

REFERENCES

Fossati, D. 2017. From periphery to centre: local government and the emergence of universal healthcare in Indonesia. *Contemporary Southeast Asia: A Journal of International and Strategic Affairs*, 39(1): 178–203.

Fossati, D. 2022. *Unity through Division: Political Islam, Representation and Democracy in Indonesia*. Cambridge University Press.

Fossati, D. 2024a. Illiberal resistance to democratic backsliding: the case of radical political Islam in Indonesia. *Democratization*, 31(3): 616–637.

Fossati, D. 2024b. *Reassessing Political Polarization and Democratic Development in Southeast Asia*, https://doi.org/10.2139/ssrn.4894284

Fossati, D. and Martinez i Coma, F. 2023. *The Meaning of Democracy in Southeast Asia: Liberalism, Egalitarianism and Participation*. Cambridge University Press.

Fossati, D., Muhtadi, B. and Warburton, E. 2022. Why democrats abandon democracy: evidence from four survey experiments. *Party Politics*, 28(3): 554–566.

Franzoni, J. and Sánchez-Ancochea, D. 2024. Emergency responses to COVID-19 and opportunities for inclusive social policy. *Journal of Social Policy*, advance online publication, https://doi.org/10.1017/S0047279424000291

Fraser, D. 2022. The economic impact of the COVID-19 pandemic on Southeast Asia. *Southeast Asia and COVID-19*, https://southeastasiacovid.asiasociety.org/the-economic-impact-of-the-covid-19-pandemic-on-southeast-asia

Gadarian, S., Goodman, S.W. and Pepinsky, T.B. 2021. Partisanship, health behavior, and policy attitudes in the early stages of the COVID-19 pandemic. *PLoS One*, 16(4): e0249596, https://doi.org/10.1371/journal.pone.0249596

Galasso, V., Pons, V., Profeta, P., Becher, M., Brouard, S. and Foucault, M. 2020. Gender differences in COVID-19 attitudes and behavior: panel evidence from eight countries. *Proceedings of the National Academy of Sciences*, 117(44): 27285–27291.

Garcia, S. 2024. "Local Going National": The Rise of Provincial Outsiders to the Presidency in Indonesia and the Philippines. PhD thesis Submitted to Department of Public and International Affairs. (July).

Gawronski, V. and Olson, R. 2013. Disasters as crisis triggers for critical junctures? The 1976 Guatemala Case. *Latin American Politics and Society*, 55(2): 133–149.

Giattino, C., Ritchie, H., Rodés-Guirao, L., Appel, C., Gavrilov, D., Giattino, C. et al. 2024. Excess mortality during the Coronavirus pandemic (COVID-19). *Our World in Data*, https://ourworldindata.org/excess-mortality-covid

Glaser, H. 2021. *Thailand's Covid-19 Struggle: Conditions, Consequences, Revelations*. Hans Seidel Stiftung, www.hss.de/fileadmin/user_upload/HSS/Dokumente/Weltweit_aktiv/Thailand_s_Covid-19_Struggle__Conditions_Consequences__Revelations.pdf

Gonzales, C. 2021. Duterte to Gordon: inciting to sedition? File a case and I'll sue you too. *Philippine Daily Inquirer* (16 September), https://newsinfo.inquirer.net/1488691/duterte-to-gordon-inciting-to-sedition-file-a-case-and-ill-sue-you-too

Greve, B., Blomquist, P., Hvinden, B., and van Gerven, M. 2021. Nordic welfare states – still standing or changed by the COVID-19 crisis? *Social Policy and Administration*, 55(2): 295–311.

Groeling, T. and Baum, M. 2008. Crossing the water's edge: elite rhetoric, media coverage, and the rally-round-the-flag phenomenon. *The Journal of Politics*, 70(4): 1065–1085.

Habermas, J. 2015. *The Lure of Technocracy*. Trans Ciaran Cronin, Polity Press.

Haggard, S. and Kaufman, R. 2021. *Backsliding: Democratic Regress in the Contemporary World*. Cambridge University Press.

Hajnal, G., Jeziorska, I. and Kovács, É.M. 2021. Understanding drivers of illiberal entrenchment at critical junctures: institutional responses to COVID-19 in Hungary and Poland. *International Review of Administrative Sciences*, 87(3): 612–630.

REFERENCES

Han, K. 2020. Singapore is trying to forget migrant workers are people: the outbreak in crowded dorms has brought out the city-state's prejudices. *Foreign Policy* (6 May), https://foreignpolicy.com/2020/05/06/singapore-coronavirus-pandemic-migrant-workers

Han, Q., Zheng, B., Cristea, M., Agostini, M., Bélanger, J.J., Gützkow, B. et al. 2023. Trust in government regarding COVID-19 and its associations with preventive health behaviour and prosocial behaviour during the pandemic: a cross-sectional and longitudinal study. *Psychological Medicine*, 53(1): 149–159.

Hapal, K. 2021. The Philippines' COVID-19 response: securitizing the pandemic and disciplining the pasaway. *Journal of Current Southeast Asian Affairs*, 140(2): 224–244.

Hartley, K. and Jarvis, D. 2020. Policymaking in a low-trust state: legitimacy, state capacity, and responses to COVID-19 in Hong Kong. *Policy and Society*, 39(3): 403–423.

Hay, C. and Wincott, D. 1998. Structure, agency and historical institutionalism. *Political Studies*, 46(5): 951–957.

Haydu, J. 2010. Reversals of fortune: path dependency problem solving and temporal cases. *Theory and Society*, 39(1): 25–48.

Hegewald, S., and Schraff, D. 2024. Who rallies around the flag? Evidence from panel data during the Covid-19 pandemic. *Journal of Elections, Public Opinion and Parties*, 34(1): 158–179.

Hess, S. 2016. Sources of authoritarian resilience in regional protest waves: the post-communist colour revolutions and 2011 Arab uprisings. *Government and Opposition*, 51(1): 1–29.

Hewison, K. and Rodan, G. 2011. Southeast Asia: the Left and the rise of bourgeois opposition. In R. Robison (ed), *Routledge Handbook of Southeast Asian Politics*. Routledge, 20–39.

Hipp, L., Buenning, M. and Sauermann, A. 2020. Problems and pitfalls of retrospective survey questions in COVID-19 studies. *Survey Research Methods*, 14(2): 109–114.

Hosen, N. 2023. The hunger games: Indonesia's problematic electoral system will continue in 2024. *Indonesia at Melbourne* (28 June), https://indonesiaatmelbourne.unimelb.edu.au/the-hunger-games-indonesias-problematic-electoral-system-will-continue-in-2024

Howard, C. 2001. Bureaucrats in the social policy process: administrative policy entrepreneurs and the case of working nation. *Australian Journal of Public Administration*, 60(3): 56–65.

Hutchcroft, P. and Weena, G. 2022. Strong-arming, weak steering: central-local relations in the Philippines in the era of the pandemic. *Philippine Political Science Journal*, 43(2): 123–167.

Hwang, G. 2020. The political economy of welfare in Singapore: explaining continuity and change. *Policy Studies*, 41(1): 63–79.

Iglesias, S. 2022. Violence and impunity: democratic backsliding in the Philippines and the 2022 election. *Pacific Affairs*, 95(3): 575–593.

Indra, R. 2024. Indonesian govt lost billions in social aid distribution corruption scandal: KPK. *The Star* (28 June), www.thestar.com.my/aseanplus/aseanplus-news/2024/06/28/indonesian-govt-lost-billions-in-social-aid-distribution-corruption-scandal-kpk

Indrawati, S., Satiawan, E. and Abdurohman, A. 2024. Indonesia's fiscal policy in the aftermath of the pandemic. *Bulletin of Indonesian Economic Studies*, 60(1): 1–33.

Inland Revenue Authority (Singapore). 2022. More than $28.1 billion disbursed under jobs support scheme since February 2020 (29 March), www.iras.gov.sg/news-events/newsroom/more-than-28.1-billion-disbursed-under-jobs-support-scheme-since-february-2020

Institute of Global Health Innovation. 2021. ICL Yougov Covid-19 Behaviour Tracker, https://public.tableau.com/app/profile/ighi/viz/ICLYouGovCovid-19Tracker_V0_3/1Specificpreventativebehaviourbycountry

International Crisis Group. 2024. Calming the long war in the Philippine countryside. *Asia Report*, 338 (19 April), www.crisisgroup.org/asia/south-east-asia/philippines/338-calming-long-war-philippine-countryside

International Monetary Fund. 2023. Central government debt. *Global Debt Database*, www.imf.org/external/datamapper/CG_DEBT_GDP@GDD/SWE

IPSOS. 2023. *State of the Malaysian Healthcare System: Health Service Monitor 2023* (October), www.ipsos.com/sites/default/files/ct/news/documents/2023-10/%5BIpsos%20Press%20Release%5D%20Health%20Service%20Monitor%202023_05%20Oct%202023.pdf

REFERENCES

James, K. 2022. The struggle for Singapore's Chinese heartland: the People's Action Party versus the Workers' Party versus the Singapore Democratic Party, 1998–2013. *Asian Journal of Comparative Politics*, 7(2): 233–250.

Jaoude, T. 2022. The grey areas of political illegitimacy. *Third World Quarterly*, 43(10): 2413–2429.

Jaspers, E., Lubbers, M. and De Graff, N.D. 2009. Measuring once twice: an evaluation of recalling attitudes in survey research. *European Sociological Review*, 25(3): 287–301.

Jing, Y. 2021. Seeking opportunities from crisis? China's governance responses to the COVID-19 pandemic. *International Review of Administrative Sciences*, 87(3): 631–650.

Jones, G. 2023. Impact of COVID-19 on mortality in Asia. *Asian Population Studies*, 19(2): 131–147.

Kaltwasser, C. and Zanotti, L. 2021. Populism and the welfare state. In B. Geve (ed), *Handbook on Austerity, Populism and the Welfare State*. Edward Elgar, 41–53.

Kamkhaji, J. and Radaelli, C. 2017. Crisis, learning and policy change in the European Union. *Journal of European Public Policy*, 24(5): 714–734.

Ketola, M. and Nordensvard, J. 2018. Reviewing the relationship between social policy and the contemporary populist radical right: welfare chauvinism, welfare nation state and social citizenship. *Journal of International and Comparative Social Policy*, 34(3): 172–187.

Khor, S. 2020. Why is Southeast Asia responding differently to COVID-19? *Think Global Health* (28 February), www.thinkglobalhealth.org/article/why-southeast-asia-responding-differently-covid-19

Kim, H. and Niederdeppe, J. 2013. The role of emotional response during an H1N1 influenza pandemic on a college campus. *Journal of Public Relations Research*, 25(1): 30–50.

Kim, T. 2024. Did the COVID-19 pandemic fuel public support for social protection? *Journal of Social Policy*, https://doi.org/10.1017/S004727942400014X

Kitschelt, H. 2000. Linkages between citizens and politicians in democratic polities. *Comparative Political Studies*, 33(6/7): 845–879.

Koenig, E. 2016. The three institutionalisms and institutional dynamics: understanding endogenous and exogenous change. *Journal of Public Policy*, 36(4): 639–664.

Kongkirati, P. 2024. *Thailand: Contestation, Polarization, and Democratic Regression*. Cambridge University Press.

Korpi, W. 2006. Power resources and employer-centered approaches in explanations of welfare states and varieties of capitalism: protagonists, consenters, and antagonists. *World Politics*, 58(2): 167–206.

Korpi, W. 2018. *The Democratic Class Struggle*. Routledge.

Kriesi, H., Grande, E., Lachat, R., Dolezal, M., Bornschier, S. and Frey, T. 2006. Globalization and the transformation of the national political space: six European countries compared. *European Journal of Political Research*, 45(6): 921–956.

Ku, Y. and Yeh, C. 2006. Social policy responses and social development during and after the unequal pandemic. *Asia Pacific Journal of Social Work and Development*, 32(3): 161–169.

Lal, A., Erondu, N.A., Heymann, D.L., Gitahi, G. and Yates, R. 2021. Fragmented health systems in COVID-19: rectifying the misalignment between global health security and universal health coverage. *The Lancet*, 397(10268): 61–67.

Lam, W. and Chan, K. 2015. How authoritarianism intensifies punctuated equilibrium: the dynamics of policy attention in Hong Kong. *Governance*, 28(4): 549–570.

Laohabut, T. and McCargo, D. 2024. Thailand's Movement Party: the evolution of the Move Forward Party. *Journal of East Asian Studies*, 24(1): 25–47.

Larsson, T. 2013. The strong and the weak: ups and downs of state capacity in Southeast Asia. *Asian Politics & Policy*, 5: 337–358.

Lasco, G. 2020. Medical populism and the COVID-19 pandemic. *Global Public Health*, 15(10): 1417–1429.

Laufer, A. and Bitton, M. 2021. Gender differences in the reaction to COVID-19. *Women & Health*, 61(8): 800–810.

Lemarchand, R. and Legg, K. 1972. Political clientelism and development: a preliminary analysis. *Comparative Politics*, 4(2): 149–172.

REFERENCES

Lerner, H. 2013. Permissive constitutions: democracy and religious freedom in India, Indonesia, Israel, and Turkey. *World Politics*, 65(4): 609–655.

London, J. 2014. Welfare regimes in China and Vietnam. *Journal of Contemporary Asia*, 44(1): 84–107.

Lorch, J. 2018. *Civil Society and Mirror Images of Weak States: Bangladesh and the Philippines. Governance and Limited Statehood.* Palgrave Macmillan.

Ma, S. 2007. Political science at the edge of chaos? The paradigmatic implications of historical institutionalism. *International Political Science Review*, 28(1): 57–78.

Ma, S. 2012. Power accidents and institutional changes: the case of a Chinese hospital in Hong Kong. *Continuity and Change*, 27(1): 151–174.

Mahoney, J. and Thelen, K. 2010. *A Theory of Gradual Institutional Change*. Cambridge University Press.

Marien, S. and Hooghe, M. 2011. Does political trust matter? An empirical investigation into the relation between political trust and support for law compliance. *European Journal of Political Research*, 50(2): 267–291.

Maude, R. 2020. COVID-19, government and security in Southeast Asia. *Southeast Asia and COVID-19*, https://southeastasiacovid.asia society.org/covid-19-government-and-security-in-southeast-asia

Mendoza, R. 2021. Popularity vs. performance. *Rappler* (26 August), www.rappler.com/voices/thought-leaders/opinion-popularity-vs-performance-rejoinder-duterte-reform-legacy/

Mietzner, M. 2020. Populist anti-scientism, religious polarisation, and institutionalised corruption: how Indonesia's democratic decline shaped its COVID-19 response. *Journal of Current Southeast Asian Affairs*, 39(2): 227–249.

Mietzner, M. 2021. *Democratic Deconsolidation in Southeast Asia*. Cambridge University Press.

Migdal, J. 2001. *State in Society: Studying How States and Societies Transform and Constitute One Another*. Cambridge University Press.

Ministry of Finance (Indonesia). 2021. *Fiscal & Economic Updates September 2021*, https://fiskal.kemenkeu.go.id/files/red/file/1633316561_final_fpa_red_september_compressed.pdf

Ministry of Finance (Singapore). 2020. *Advancing as One Singapore*. www.mof.gov.sg/docs/librariesprovider3/budget2020/statements/fy2020_budget_statement.pdf

Ministry of Finance (Singapore). 2021. *An Interim Assessment of the Impact of Key COVID-19 Budget Measures* (19 February), www.mof.gov.sg/docs/default-source/default-document-library/news-and-publications/featured-reports/interim-assessment---covid-19-budget-measures-(19-feb-2021).pdf

Ministry of Trade and Industry. 2021. *Economic Survey of Singapore 2020*, www.mti.gov.sg/Resources/Economic-Survey-of-Singapore/2020/Economic-Survey-of-Singapore-2020

Moffitt, B. 2016. *The Global Rise of Populism: Performance, Political Style, and Representation*. Stanford University Press.

Mok, K., Ku, Y.-W. and Yuda, T.K. 2021. Managing the COVID-19 pandemic crisis and changing welfare regimes. *Journal of Asian Public Policy*, 14(1), https://doi.org/10.1080/17516234.2020.1861722

Moreira, A. and Hick, R. 2021. COVID-19, the Great Recession and social policy: is this time different? *Social Policy & Administration*, 55(2): 261–279.

Morgenbesser, L. 2019. Cambodia's transition to hegemonic authoritarianism. *Journal of Democracy*, 30(1): 158–171.

Müller, J. 2017. *What is Populism?* University of Pennsylvania Press.

Natali, D. 2022. COVID-19 and the opportunity to change the neoliberal agenda: evidence from socio-employment policy responses across Europe. *Transfer: European Review of Labour and Research*, 28(1): 15–30.

Neelkantan, V. 2023. History of pandemics in Southeast Asia: a return of national anxieties. *Isis*, 114(S1): S419–S446.

Ngiam, J., Chew, N., Tham, S.M., Beh, D.L., Lim, Z.Y., Li, T.Y.W. et al. 2021. Demographic shift in COVID-19 patients in Singapore from an aged, at-risk population to young migrant workers with reduced risk of severe disease. *International Journal of Infectious Disease*, 103: 329–335.

REFERENCES

Nichols, C. and Myers, A. 2010. Exploiting the opportunity for reconstructive leadership: presidential responses to enervated political regimes. *American Politics Research*, 38(5): 806–841.

OECD (Organisation for Economic Co-operation and Development). 2022. *Society at a Glance: Asia/Pacific 2022*. OECD Publishing.

OECD (Organisation for Economic Co-operation and Development). 2025. *OECD Economic Outlook – Tackling Uncertainty, Reviving Growth*. OECD Publishing.

Oliver, S. and Ostwald, K. 2020. Singapore's pandemic election: opposition parties and valence politics in GE2020. *Pacific Affairs*, 93(4): 759–780.

Ortiz-Ospina, E., Roser, M. and Arrigada, P. 2016. Trust: how does interpersonal trust differ across societies and what role does it play in shaping economic development? *Our World in Data*, https://ourworldindata.org/trust

Orton, M. and Sarkar, S. 2023. COVID-19 and (mis) understanding public attitudes to social security: re-setting debate. *Critical Social Policy*, 43(1): 3–28.

Panneerselvam, I. and Tayeb, A. 2023. Protesting in the time of pandemic: diagonal accountability, #KerajaanGagal, and democratic regression in Malaysia. *Journal of Current Southeast Asian Affairs*, 42(3): 421–440.

Parmanand, S. 2020. The dangers of masculinity contests in a time of pandemic. *Oxford Political Review* (18 April), https://oxfordpoliticalreview.com/2020/04/18/the-dangers-of-masculinity-contests-in-a-time-of-pandemic

Pepinsky, T. 2024. Indonesia's election reveals its democratic challenges. *Brookings* (12 January), www.brookings.edu/articles/indonesias-election-reveals-its-democratic-challenges/

Peters, D. and Youssef, F. 2016. Public trust in the healthcare system in a developing country. *International Journal of Health Planning and Management*, 31(2): 227–241.

Petter, P. and Howard, C. 2024. Do crisis narratives encourage redistribution? Australian housing policy debates during COVID-19. *Journal of Social Policy*, https://doi.org/10.1017/S0047279424000242

Piedad, M. 2023. Under the knife: the 2024 health budget. *Ibon* (8 September), www.ibon.org/2024p-health-cuts/

Pongcharoensuk, P., Adisasmito, W., Sat, M., Silkavute, P., Muchlisoh, L., Cong Hoat, P. and Coker, R. 2021. Avian and pandemic human influenza policy in South-East Asia: the interface between economic and public health imperatives. *Health Policy and Planning*, 27(5): 374–383.

Poolsuwan, S. 1995. Malaria in prehistoric Southeastern Asia. *Southeast Asian Journal of Tropical Medicine and Public Health*, 26(1): 3–22.

Purnamasari, R. and Ahmad, Z. 2021. Malaysian households during COVID-19: fading resilience, rising vulnerability. *World Bank Blogs* (27 October), https://blogs.worldbank.org/en/eastasiapacific/malaysian-households-during-covid-19-fading-resilience-rising-vulnerability

Rahim, L. and Yeoh, L. 2019. Social policy reform and rigidity in Singapore's authoritarian developmental state. In L. Rahim and M. Barr (eds), *The Limits of Authoritarian Governance in Singapore's Developmental State*. Palgrave Macmillan, 95–130.

Ramesh, M. and Bali, A. 2021. Thailand: universal health care under government stewardship. *Health Policy in Asia: A Policy Design Approach*. Cambridge University Press, 130–148.

Rappler. 2022. Richard Gordon, Leila de Lima headed for reelection loss (10 May), www.rappler.com/philippines/elections/results-richard-gordon-de-lima-reelection-bids-2022/

Rathore, F. and Farooq, F. 2020. Information overload and infodemic in the COVID-19 pandemic. *Journal of the Pakistan Medical Association*, 70(5): S162–S165.

Reid, J., Brown, S.J. and Dmello, J. 2023. COVID-19, diffuse anxiety, and public (mis)trust in government: empirical insights and implications for crime and justice. *Criminal Justice Review*, 27: 1–18.

Reuters. 2020. Indonesia confirms first cases of coronavirus. *Bangkok Post* (2 March), www.reuters.com/article/world/indonesia-confirms-first-cases-of-coronavirus-link-to-japanese-visitor-idUSKBN20P0HD/

REFERENCES

Reuters. 2022. Pandemic pushed millions more into poverty in the Philippines, government says (15 August), www.reuters.com/world/asia-pacific/pandemic-pushed-millions-more-into-poverty-philippines-govt-2022-08-15/#:~:text=The%20number%20of%20people%20living,target%20of%2015.5%25%2D17.5%25

Rinscheid, A., Eberlein, B., Emmenegger, P. and Schneider, V. 2020. Why do junctures become critical? Political discourse, agency, and joint belief shifts in comparative perspective. *Regulation & Governance*, 14: 653–673.

Roberts, C. and Geels, F. 2019. Conditions for politically accelerated transitions: historical institutionalism the multi-level perspective and two historical case studies in transport and agriculture. *Technological Forecasting & Social Change*, 140: 221–240.

Rodan, G. 2009. Accountability and suthoritarianism: human rights in Malaysia and Singapore. *Journal of Contemporary Asia*, 39(2): 180–203.

Rodan, G. 2022. *Civil Society in Southeast Asia: Power Struggles and Political Regimes*, Cambridge University Press.

Ru, H., Yang, E. and Zu, K. 2021. Combating the COVID-19 pandemic: the role of the SARS imprint, *Management Science*, 67(9): 5606–5615.

Rudolph, T. and Evans, J. 2005. Political trust, ideology, and public support for government spending. *American Journal of Political Science*, 49(3): 660–671.

Ruisch, B.C., Moore, C., Granados Samayoa, J., Boggs, S., Ladanyi, J. and Fazio, R. 2021. Examining the left-right divide through the lens of a global crisis: ideological differences and their implications for responses to the COVID-19 pandemic. *Political Psychology*, 42(5): 795–816.

Saransomrurtai, C. and Reinhart, R. 2020. Pandemic highlights gaps in trust in Southeast Asia. *Gallup Blog* (9 April), https://news.gallup.com/opinion/gallup/307985/pandemic-highlights-gaps-trust-southeast-asia.aspx

Schnose, V. 2015. Who is in charge here? Legislators, bureaucrats and the policy making process. *Party Politics*, 23(4): 342–363.

Sciortino, R. (ed). 2023. *Who Cares? COVID-19 Social Response in Southeast Asia*. Silkworm Books.

Scott, J.C. 1972. Patron-client politics and political change in Southeast Asia. *American Political Science Review*, 66(1): 91–113.

Selway, J.S. 2011. Electoral reform and public policy outcomes in Thailand: the politics of the 30-baht health scheme. *World Politics*, 63(1): 165–202.

Setijadi, C. 2021. The pandemic as political opportunity: Jokowi's Indonesia in the time of Covid-19. *Bulletin of Indonesian Economic Studies*, 57(3): 297–320.

Shim, J. 2024. Shadow of a critical juncture. In J. Shim (ed), *Mass-Elite Representation Gap in Old and New Democracies: Critical Junctures and Elite Agency*. University of Michigan Press, 91–114.

Shin, H.B., Mckenzie, M. and Oh, D.Y. 2022. *Covid-19 in Southeast Asia: Insights for a Post-Pandemic World*. LSE Press.

Simmons, B. 2000. International law and state behavior: commitment and compliance in international monetary affairs. *The American Political Science Review*, 94(4), 819–835.

Sinpeng, A. 2021. Hashtag activism: social media and the #FreeYouth protests in Thailand. *Critical Asian Studies*, 53(2): 192–205.

Sit, D. 2022. *Post-Covid Prospects: Indonesia: Interview with Slamet Noegroho, Consul for Economic Affairs of Indonesia in Hong Kong*. Hong Kong Trade and Development Council (10 January), https://research.hktdc.com/en/article/OTU0ODAxNjgw

Slater, D. 2010. Altering authoritarianism: institutional complexity and autocratic agency in Indonesia. In J. Mahoney and K. Thelen (eds), *Explaining Institutional Agency, and Power*. Cambridge University Press, 132–167.

Slater, D. and Simmons, E. 2010. Informative regress: critical antecedents in comparative politics. *Comparative Political Studies*, 43(7): 886–917.

Snipes A. and Mudde, C. 2020. 'France's (kinder, gentler) extremist': Marine Le Pen, intersectionality, and media framing of female populist radical right leaders. *Politics & Gender*, 16(2): 438–470.

Soifer, H. 2012. The causal logic of critical junctures. *Comparative Political Studies*, 45(12): 1572–1597.

REFERENCES

Sorenson, A. 2023. Taking critical junctures seriously: theory and method for causal analysis of rapid institutional change. *Planning Perspectives*, 38(5): 929–947.

Straits Times. 2025. GE2025: GST hike was implemented with 'great care', opposition ignored facts to maximise votes, says PM Wong (28 April), https://www.straitstimes.com/singapore/politics/pm-wong-says-gst-hike-was-implemented-with-great-care-opposition-ignored-facts-to-maximise-votes?utm_medium=social&utm_source=facebook&utm_campaign=stfb

Tagliacozzo, E. 2014. Pilgrim ships and the frontiers of contagion: quarantine regimes from Southeast Asia to the Red Sea. In T. Harper and S. Amrith (eds), *Histories of Health in Southeast Asia: Perspectives on the Long Twentieth Century*. Indiana University Press, 47–60.

Tan, K.P. 2010. *Singapore: A Depoliticized Civil Society in a Dominant-Party System?* Briefing Paper No 3: 1–4 for the Friedrich Ebert Stiftung, https://library.fes.de/pdf-files/bueros/china/11396.pdf

Tan, K. 2012. The ideology of pragmatism: neo-liberal globalisation and political authoritarianism in Singapore. *Journal of Contemporary Asia*, 42(1): 67–92.

Tan, K. and Chan, S. 2023. *Populations and Precarity During the COVID-19 Pandemic: Southeast Asian Perspectives*. ISEAS–Yusof Ishak Institute.

Tan, N. and Preece, C. 2024. Democratic backsliding in illiberal Singapore. *Asian Journal of Comparative Politics*, 9(1): 25–49.

Tayles, N. and Buckley, H. 2004. Leprosy and tuberculosis in Iron Age Southeast Asia? *American Journal of Biological Anthropology*, 125(3): 239–256.

Teehankee, J. 2020. Duterte's COVID-19 powers and the paradox of the Philippine presidency. *CSEAS COVID-19 Chronicles* (28 April), https://covid-19chronicles.cseas.kyoto-u.ac.jp/en/post-007-html

Teehankee, J. and Thompson, M. 2016. The vote in the Philippines: electing a strongman. *Journal of Democracy*, 27(4): 125–134.

Thaler, K. 2022. Civil wars as critical junctures: theoretical grounding and empirical applications. *APSA Preprints*, https://doi.org/10.33774/apsa-2022-drtz3

The Economist. 2024. Estimated cumulative excess deaths per 100,000 people during COVID (17 June). *Our World in Data*, https://ourworldindata.org/grapher/excess-deaths-cumulative-per-100k-economist

Thelen, K. 1999. Historical institutionalism in comparative politics, *Annual Review of Political Science*, 2: 369–404.

Thomas, N. 2006. The regionalization of avian influenza in East Asia: responding to the next pandemic(?). *Asian Survey*, 46(6): 917–936.

Thompson, M. 2021. Duterte's violent populism: mass murder, political legitimacy and the 'death of development' in the Philippines. *Journal of Contemporary Asia*, 52(3): 403–428.

Thompson, M. 2022. Brute force governance: public approval despite policy failure during the COVID-19 pandemic in the Philippines. *Journal of Current Southeast Asian Affairs*, 41(3): 399–421.

Thompson, M. 2023. *The Philippines: From 'People Power' to Democratic Backsliding*. Cambridge University Press.

Thompson, M. and Cheng, E. 2022. Transgressing taboos: discursive radicalization among youth activists in networked protest movements in Hong Kong and Thailand. *Social Movement Studies*, 22(5–6): 802–821.

Tonelli, S., Harris, E. and Deeg, F. 2024. Cross-class solidarity in times of crisis: the economic impact of the COVID-19 pandemic on support for redistribution. *Journal of European Social Policy*, 34(5): 556–572.

Touchton, M., Knaul, F.M., McDonald, T. and Frenk, J. 2023. The perilous mix of populism and pandemics: lessons from COVID-19. *Social Sciences*, 12(7): 1–9.

Trantidis, A. 2016. *Clientelism and Economic Policy: Greece and the Crisis*. Routledge.

Tze, K.S. 2016. Beware the welfarism trap. *The Straits Times* (20 January), www.straitstimes.com/opinion/beware-the-welfarism-trap

REFERENCES

Van Bavel, J., Cichocka, A., Carraro, V. and Sjåstad, H. 2022. National identity predicts public health support during a global pandemic. *Nature Communications*, 13(1): art 517, https://doi.org/0.1038/s41467-021-27668-9

Wang, H., Paulson, K.R., Pease, S.A., Watson, S., Comfort, H., Zheng, P. et al. 2022. Estimating excess mortality due to the COVID-19 pandemic: a systematic analysis of COVID-19-related mortality, 2020–21. *The Lancet*, 399(10334): 1513–1536.

Warburton, E. 2016. Indonesian Politics in 2016: Jokowi and the New Developmentalism. *Bulletin of Indonesian Economic Studies* 52(3): 297–320.

Wayland, K. 2008. Toward a new theory of institutional change. *World Politics*, 60(2): 281–314.

Weiss, M. 2022. Is Malaysian democracy backsliding or merely staying put? *Asian Journal of Comparative Politics*, 9(1): 9–24.

Welsh, B. 2016. Clientelism and control: PAP's fight for safety in GE2015. *The Round Table*, 105(2): 119–128.

White, S. and Liu, X. 2005. Financing new ventures in China: system antecedents and institutionalization. *Research Policy*, 34(6): 894–913.

Williamson, O. 1998. The institutions of governance. *The American Economic Review*, 88(2): 75–79.

Wiwad, D., Mercier, B., Piff, P.K., Shariff, A. and Aknin, L.B. 2021. Recognizing the impact of COVID-19 on the poor alters attitudes towards poverty and inequality. *Journal of Experimental Social Psychology*, 93: art 104083, https://doi.org/10.1016/j.jesp.2020.104083

Woo, J. 2020. Policy capacity and Singapore's response to the COVID-19 pandemic. *Policy and Society*, 39(3): 345–362.

World Bank. 2020. Impacts of COVID-19 on households in the Philippines: results from the Philippines COVID-19 Households Survey, Round 2 – December 2020, https://thedocs.worldbank.org/en/doc/ab24c2a718fb53a344c5942d236b2fe6-0070062021/original/Philippines-COVID-19-High-Frequency-Survey-Household-Results-Slides.pdf

World Bank Group. 2023. *Bridging the Gap: Inequality and Jobs in Thailand*. World Bank Group, https://documents1.worldbank.org/curated/en/099112823133018003/pdf/P17759905901d70ed0a968052455d5252f0.pdf?_gl=1*1pgnpyi*_gcl_au*ODQwODMxNTcwLjE3MjMyOTM2ODE

Yuda, T., Kim, M., Pholpark, A. and Bin Aedy Rahman, H.N. 2022. Unmasking the social policy responses of COVID-19 in four Southeast Asian Nations: institutional patterns and policy adjustment. *Asia Pacific Journal of Social Work and Development*, 32(4): 294–317.

Index

References to figures appear in *italic* type; those in **bold** type refer to tables. Reference to notes show the page number, note number and chapter number (119n1 (ch1)).

A

activism 6, 10, 78–79, 93–94
age
  attitudinal change 57–58, *59*, **60**, 62
  behavioural change **71**
  COVID-19 impact 80–81
  respondent demographics 47, **50**
AIDS 16, 17
An, B. 21
antecedent conditions 28, 29, 30, 32, 42, 78, 100
anti-welfarism
  overview 6, 37, 105, 111
  Singapore 7, 83–84, 92–93
anxiety *see* infection anxiety
Arguelles, C. 88
Aslam, M. 8
Aspinall, E.et al. 21
Association of Southeast Asian Nations (ASEAN) 15–17, 18, **18**
attitudinal change
  conclusions 75, 103–104, 108–109, 110, 111, 112, 113
  individual-level variables 33–35
  research aim 45–46
  survey findings **51**, 52–58, **54**, *56*, *57*, *59*, **60–61**, 62–66, *66*, 70
  survey prompts 46–48

Australia 110
authoritarianism
  change theories 35, 41
  Europe 114
  Malaysia 10, 99
  Singapore 10, 11, 83
  Southeast Asia overview 6, 9–10, 19, 107, 113
  Thailand 12

B

Barisian Sosialis 10
Baswedan, Anies 92
Bates, G. et al. 106
Batuba, Juliari 92
behavioural change
  individual-level factors 33–35
  research aim 45–46
  survey findings 67–70, *68*, **71–72**, 73–75, *73*, 103
  survey prompts 47
Belgium 111
bias 45–46, 67
border restrictions 21, 33, 81, 86–87
Brunei **18**, 119n1 (ch1)

C

Cambodia 10, **18**, 119n1 (ch1)
Canada 111

Capoccia, G. 26, 29, 42
Chan, K. 35
Chan, S. 8
change agents
  examples 36–37
  marginalisation 6, 78–80, 100, 105, 112, 113
Chen, H. et al. 41
childcare services 46, **54**, 75, 119n1 (ch3)
China 16, 18
Christianity 12, **116**
civil society
  change theories 36, 39
  pre-existing protests 93–94, 97–98, 99
  Southeast Asia overview 6, 10, 11, 16, 17, 19
  weakening 78–80, 86, 87, 105, 107, 113
clientelism 6, 38, 85, 90, 113
coalition formation 40, 79, 93–95, 99, 100, 113
communism 9–10, 78
conservative ideology
  Europe 114
  individual-level factors 34
  Indonesia 85
  Malaysia 77, 93, 99, 100
  Singapore 53, 100
  Southeast Asia conclusions 100, 104, 105, 107, 108, 113
  Southeast Asia introduction 6, 10
  Thailand 77, 93, 98, 100
contact tracing 80, 86
corruption 84, 85, 90–92, 98
Corruption Eradication Commission (KPK) 91
COVID-19, Southeast Asia overview 17–21, **18**
COVID-19 exposure levels
  research findings **50**, **60**, 62–63, **71**, 73, 75, 103
  survey prompts 48, 49
critical junctures
  institutional change model 26–32, 35–36, 39–42
  research findings 76–77, 78, 100, 101, 102, 106–107, 112
  crowd avoidance 47, 68, *68*, 69

D

death rates 18, **18**, 80, 86, 87, 93, 97
democratic backsliding 6, 10–11, 79, 84–85, 87, 100, 113
democratisation 6, 9, 78–79
drugs, illegal 79, 84, 86
Duterte, Rodrigo R. 79, 84–86, 88, 89, 90–91

E

Ebbinghaus, B. et al. 108
economic growth
  COVID-19 impact 20–21, 77, 80–81, 93, 95–96, 98–99
  Southeast Asia overview 6, 9, 14, 107
economic redistribution
  attitudinal change **54**, 55, **60**, 65–66, *66*, 75, 119n1 (ch3)
  behavioural change 70, **71**
  change theories 36, 37
  COVID-19 policies 77, 80–83, 86–87, 89–90, 95–99
  Southeast Asia overview 7, 9, 12
  survey prompts 47, **51**
education for workers 46, **54**, 119n1 (ch3)
education levels
  attitudinal change 57, 58, *59*, **61**, 62, 66
  behavioural change **72**
  Malaysian recovery 96
  respondent sociodemographics 47, **50**, **116**
elections
  Malaysia 10, 79, 94–95, 99
  overview 35
  Philippines 91
  Singapore 79, 81, 84
  Thailand 79, 93–94, 98
Emmenegger, P. 40, 41

emotional responses 27, 34, 57, 63, 70, 73
see also infection anxiety
Europe 15, 107, 108, 109, 111, 114

F

Fealy, G. 87
Feitelson, E. 40
fiscal stability 7, 20, 37, 83
fiscal stimulus packages 3, 20, 82, 88, 89
Foa, R. 88
freedoms, suspension of 21, 34, 79
Future Forward Party 94, 98

G

gender
  attitudinal change 57, 58, *59*, **61**, 66
  behavioural change **72**, 74
  job losses 96
  respondent demographics **50**, **116**
Germany 108, 111, 114
Glaser, H. 97
government performance, evaluations
  attitudinal change **51**, **60**, 62, 63–64, 70, 81, 109
  behavioural change **71**
government spending
  COVID-19 policies 77, 81–83, 88–92, 99
  Europe 108
  support for 64, 65
Gunaratna, R. 8

H

hand-washing 47, 68–69, *68*
Hapal, K. 85
health insurance 5, 46, **54**, 75, 119n1 (ch3)
healthcare
  attitudinal change 5, 54–56, **54**, *56*, 75
  historical institutionalism 27
  Southeast Asia overview 14, 15–17
  survey prompts 46, 47
  universal systems 80, 91
Hewison, K. 10
historical institutionalism 25–27, 42, 111
HIV/AIDS 16, 17

I

Ibrahim, Anwar 99
ideological orientation *see* anti-welfarism; conservative ideology; economic redistribution; neoliberalism
immigration 38, 80, 88
income
  attitudinal change 57, 58, *59*, **61**
  behavioural change 66, **72**
  COVID-19 overview 3, 20, 109
  COVID-19 policies 82, 83, 88, 91, 95–96
  inequality 98–99
  reductions 97, 99
  respondent sociodemographics 47–48, **50**, **116**
individual-level factors, introduction 32–35
Indonesia
  attitudinal change 53, 55, *56*, 57, **60–61**, 62–66, 75
  behavioural change 68–69, *68*, **71–72**, 73, 74
  change agents, marginalisation 78, 79, 80
  COVID-19 overview **18**, 21
  COVID-19 policies 77, 84–92, 93, 100
  institutional context 7, 9, 10, 11, 12, *13*, 14
  regional health policy 16
  survey respondents 49, **116–118**
Indonesian Communist Party (PKI) 9
inequality
  attitudinal change **54**, 55, 63, 119n1 (ch3)
  critical junctures 27, 104

populism 38
Singapore 83
Southeast Asia overview 7, 14, 112
survey prompts 46–47
Thailand 98–99
infection anxiety
attitudinal change **60**, 63, 103
behavioural change **71**, 73–74, *73*, 75
individual-level factor 34, 35
respondent experiences 48, **51**
infectious diseases 15–17, 36, 41, 101–102
informal employment 14, 96
institutional change
research aim 2, 5, 12, 14
theoretical overview 25–32, 35–42
institutional trust
attitudinal change 58, **60**, 63–64, 75, 104, 105–106, 109
behavioural change 70, **71**
change theories 39
Singapore 81
Southeast Asia overview 12, *13*
survey prompts 48–49, **51**
International Monetary Fund (IMF) 20
Islam 11–12, 79, 82, 87, 99, **116**

J

job losses
attitudinal change **54**, 63, 119n1 (ch3)
behavioural change 73
figures 82, 86, 89, 96
mitigation policies 82, 89
survey prompts 46, 48
Jokowi 79, 84–85, 86–88, 89, 91–92

K

Kelemen, R. 26, 29
Ku, Y. 20

L

labour unions 6, 10, 12, 78
Lam, W. 35

Laos **18**, 36, 119n1 (ch1)
Lee Kuan Yew 81, 84
Left-wing political actors
change agents 36
populism 38
suppression of 6, 9–10, 78, 105, 107, 113, 114
local government 48, 86, 88–89
lockdowns 81, 85–87, 96, 97
low incomes
attitudinal change 57, 58, *59*
clientelism 38
COVID-19 overview 3, 20, 109
COVID-19 policies 82, 83, 88, 91, 95–96
respondent sociodemographics **116**

M

Ma, S. 26
Malaysia
attitudinal change 53, 55, *56*, *57*, **60–61**, 63, 64, 65
behavioural change 68–69, *68*, **71–72**
change agents, marginalisation 79
COVID-19 policies 77, 90, 92–97, 99
COVID-19 statistics **18**
institutional context 7, 9, 10–11, 12, *13*, 14
survey respondents 49, **116–118**
Marcos, Ferdinand E. 10
Marcos, Imee 91
marginalisation
change agents 6, 78–80, 100, 105, 112, 113
populations 3, 11, 20, 37, 38
see also vulnerable populations
mask-wearing 47, 67, 68–69, *68*
Maude, R. 19
Mietzner, M. 85
migrant workers 80, 88
military coups 10, 79, 93, 98, 119n1 (ch1)
Move Forward Party 98
Myanmar 10, **18**, 36, 119n1 (ch1)

INDEX

N

national identity
  attitudinal change 34–35, 56, **60**, 65, 75, 104, 110
  behavioural change 70, **71**
  survey prompts 49, **51**
national insurance 91
negative outcomes of critical junctures 29–30, 42–43, 76, 77, 102, 106–107
neoliberalism 6, 37, 77, 83, 100, 105
Netherlands 111
New People's Army 10
non-Western/Western country comparisons 4, 8–9, 14, 107–109, 114

P

Pakatan Harapan 94, 99
PAP (People's Action Party) 7, 9–10, 11, 80, 81, 83
Parmanand, S. 85
partisanship
  attitudinal change 34, **60**, 65–66, 109
  behavioural change 70, **71**
  survey prompts 48, **51**
path dependency 26, 102, 106
patronage networks 7, 38, 91–92, 93, 100, 105
People's Action Party (PAP) 7, 9–10, 11, 80, 81, 83
Perikatan Nasional (PN) government 94, 99
permissive conditions
  institutional change model 28–29, 30–31, 32, 39, 42
  research findings 79, 105
Pharmally scandal 90–91
Pheu Thai 93–94, 98
Philippines
  attitudinal change 53, 55, *56, 57*, **60–61**, 62–63, 66
  change agents, marginalisation 78, 79
  COVID-19 overview **18**, 21

COVID-19 policies 77, 84–92, 93, 95, 100
institutional context 7, 9, 10, 12, *13*, 14
survey respondents 49, **116–118**
PKI (Indonesian Communist Party) 9
PN (Perikatan Nasional) government 94, 99
policy compliance 12, 21, 28, 32, 34, 86
political (in)stability
  change theories 39, 40, 42
  Southeast Asia overview 9–10, 12, 100, 102
political legitimacy
  definition 39
  Malaysia 93, 94, 99, 106
  Southeast Asia overview 12, *13*, 105–106
  Thailand 93–94, 97–98, 106
populism 6–7, 37–38, 84, 87–88, 93
poverty
  attitudinal change **54**, 119n1 (ch1)
  Indonesia 89, 90
  Philippines 86, 88, 90
  Southeast Asia overview 14, 20
  survey prompts 46, 49
  Thailand 95
Prabowo Subianto 92
Pranowo, Ganjar 92
productive conditions 28, 30, 31, 32, 39, 42
progressive movements 6, 10, 78, 105, 111, 113–114

Q

qualitative case studies 2, 5
quantitative surveys 2, 5, 8, 44–49, **50–51**, 67

R

Raka, Gibran Rakabuming 92
religion 11–12, 78, 79, 82, 87, 99, **116**

respondent sociodemographics 45, 47–48, **50**, **116–118**
Rinscheid, A. et al. 30
Rodan, G. 10, 78
Romualdez, Martin 91
Ru, H. et al 41

S

Sciortino, R. 7
severe acute respiratory syndrome (SARS) 16–17, 26, 41
Shim, J. 30
Shin, H.B. et al. 7
Singapore
  attitudinal change 53, 55, 56, 57, **60–61**, 63–66, 75, 103, 109
  behavioural change 68–69, 68, **71–72**, 73, 74
  change agents, marginalisation 78, 79
  COVID-19 overview 7, **18**
  COVID-19 policies 77, 80–84, 90, 92–93, 100
  institutional context 9–11, 12, 13, 14
  regional health context 15, 16
  survey respondents 49, **116–118**
skills training 46, **54**, 82, 83, 119n1 (ch3)
social distancing 47, 67, 68, 68, 69, 81
social insurance 6, 19, 95, 96, 111, 114
socialism 6, 78
sociodemographics, respondents 45, 47–48, **50**, **116–118**
Sorenson, A. 26, 28
South Korea 108
Southeast Asia
  COVID-19 overview 17–21, **18**
  institutional context 8–14, 13
  regional health policy 15–16
  welfare state institutions 4, 5–10, 19–20, 107, 108–109, 112–113
Suharto 9

T

Tagliacozzo, E. 15
Tan, K. 8, 83
Tang, S. 21
taxation 49, 65, 82, 97
technocratic ideology 37, 77, 81, 83, 85, 92, 100
testing 80, 81, 86
Thailand
  attitudinal change 53, 55, 56, 57, **60–61**, 63–66
  behavioural change 68–69, 68, **71–72**, 73
  change agents, marginalisation 78, 79, 80
  COVID-19 overview 7, **18**, 21
  COVID-19 policies 77, 92–99, 100
  institutional context 9, 10, 11, 12, 13, 14
  regional health context 16
  survey respondents 49, **116–118**
Thaksin Shinawatra 93, 98
Thelen, K. 41
trade unions 9, 36
trust 33–34, 109
  see also institutional trust

U

unemployment 20, 21, 89, 90
unemployment benefit 3, 5, 46, **54**
United Kingdom 108, 111
United Malay National Organisation 94, 99
United States of America (USA) 34, 109, 111
United Thai Nation Party 98
universal basic income 3, 46, **54**, 119n1 (ch3)
universal healthcare 80, 91
universal minimum wage 84

V

vaccinations 3, 80, 81, 86, 87, 95, 98
Vietnam 10, 16, **18**, 119n1 (ch1)

INDEX

vulnerable populations 88, 89, 91, 95, 96, 99
see also marginalisation, populations

W

welfare state institutions
 attitudinal change 53–58, *56*, *59*, 65–66, 75, 108–109
 change theories 36–38
 COVID-19 policies 82, 88–93, 95–99
 Europe 107, 108, 109, 111, 114
 research aim 1–2

Southeast Asia overview 4, 5–10, 19–20, 107, 108–109, 112–113
Western/non-Western country comparisons 4, 8–9, 14, 107–109, 114
Widodo, Joko (Jokowi) 79, 84–85, 86–88, 89, 91–92
Wong, Lawrence 84
Workers' Party 10
working class 11, 36

Y

Yang, Michael 90
Yeh, C. 20
Yuda, T. et al. 20